Moon in a Mason Jar

AND

What My Father Believed

MOON IN A MASON JAR

and

WHAT MY FATHER BELIEVED

Two Volumes of Poetry

by Robert Wrigley

University of Illinois Press

Urbana and Chicago

© 1986, 1991, 1998 by Robert Wrigley
Manufactured in the United States of America
P 5 4 3 2 1

This book is printed on acid-free paper.

Library of Congress Cataloging-in-Publication Data

Wrigley, Robert, 1951–
   [Moon in a mason jar]
   Moon in a mason jar ; and, What my father believed :
   two volumes of poetry / by Robert Wrigley.
   p.   cm.
   ISBN 0-252-06672-3 (pbk. : alk. paper)
   I. Wrigley, Robert, 1951–   .
   II. Title.
   III. Title: What my father believed.
   PS3573.R58M6   1998
   811'.54—dc21
   97-22182
   CIP

CONTENTS

Moon in a Mason Jar

What My Father Believed

Moon in a Mason Jar

for Kim
for Philip
and with special thanks to Paul Zarzyski and Phyllis Wright

PART ONE

This is thy hour O Soul, thy free flight into the wordless,
Away from books, away from art, the day erased, the lesson done,
Thee fully forth emerging, silent, gazing, pondering the themes thou lovest best,
Night, sleep, death and the stars.

—Whitman

MOONLIGHT: CHICKENS ON THE ROAD

Called out of dream by the pitch and screech,
I awoke to see my mother's hair
set free of its pincurls, springing out
into the still and hurtling air
above the front seat and just as suddenly gone.
The space around us twisted,
and in the instant before the crash
I heard the bubbling of the chickens,
the homely racket they make at all speeds,
signifying calm, resignation, oblivion.

And I listened. All through the slash
and clatter, the rake of steel, shatter of glass,
I listened, and what came
was a blizzard moan in the wind, a wail
of wreckage, severed hoses and lives,
a storm of loose feathers, and in the final
whirl approximating calm, the cluck
and fracas of the birds. I crawled
on hands and knees where a window should
have been and rose uneven

in November dusk. Wind blew
a snow of down, and rows of it quivered along
the shoulder. One thin stream of blood
oozed, flocked in feathers.
This was in the Ozarks, on a road curving miles
around Missouri, and as far as I could
see, no light flickered through the timber,
no mail box leaned the flag
of itself toward pavement, no cars
seemed ever likely to come along.

So I walked, circled the darkening disaster
my life had come to, and cried.
I cried for my family there,
knotted in the snarl of metal and glass;
for the farmer, looking dead, half in
and half out of his windshield; and for myself,
ambling barefoot through the jeweled debris,
glass slitting little blood-stars in my soles,
my arm hung loose at the elbow
and whispering its prophecies of pain.

Around and around the tilted car
and the steaming truck, around the heap
of exploded crates, the smears and small hunks
of chicken and straw. Through
an hour of loneliness and fear
I walked, in the almost black of Ozark night,
the moon just now burning into Missouri.
Behind me, the chickens followed my lead,
some fully upright, pecking

the dim pavement for suet or seed,
some half-hobbled by their wounds, worthless wings
fluttering in the effort. The faintest
light turned their feathers phosphorescent,
and as I watched they came on, as though they believed
me some savior, some highwayman
or commando come to save them the last night
of their clucking lives. This, they must have
believed, was the end they'd always heard of,
this the rendering more efficient than the axe,

the execution more anonymous than
a wringing arm. I walked on, no longer crying,
and soon the amiable and distracted chattering came
again, a sound like chuckling, or the backward suck
of hard laughter. And we walked
to the cadence their clucking called,
a small boy towing a cloud around a scene
of death, coming round and round
like a dream, or a mountain road,
like a pincurl, like pulse, like life.

THE BEES   *for Kitty*

1

Maybe you heard them first without knowing,
some silken push and sway behind the walls,
the dim respiration of old and trusty plumbing.
And at first there seemed only a few
stragglers, lost in the maze of city blocks
and alleys, missing flights of half-dozens
daubing their pollen on the window weights,
dying in the no-man's land of dead air
behind the shades.
                    Then one day
you opened the cellar door and heard them
there, befuddled and angry, fallen out
of their intricate hives between the studs.
Soon they were all around you, heaving
in a dark mass upon the houseplants,
bobbing in a top-shaped swarm
above the rich chenille garden of the bedspread.

2

Remember the panic you pushed aside
when they came to you and wove around you
their tight electric air, fluttering
the down on your arms and ears, kissing you
lighter than any man. Remember
your only flinch, minor,
that trapped a bee against your knuckle.
And remember the pain that blossomed
below the skin there, like any true flower.

6

3

The keeper, in full dress and smoker,
aimed to take a census of the bees, but knew
as soon as you, despite his love,
the emptiness of such a number.
So he flushed them out with a garden hose
and set the cellar awash in tides of the drowned.
A few honeyed drops bled through your walls,
and the bees were gone.
                              That first night
was the stillest you ever heard. The elderly walls
creaked, the toilet murmured for hours.
You thought you'd never sleep in that brittle quiet,
in a house that held its breath
and made you hold yours, thinking
every twitch a bee's dark kiss,
every breath a buzzing.

NIGHTCRAWLERS   *for Paul Zarzyski*

          1

It rains for three days
and out of the ground come worms,
nightcrawlers collared in puddles, caught
too shallow in the mad perc of a cloudburst,
heading for the high country
of sidewalks, the towering crowns of backstreets.
One monster, a foot long, slithers under the back door
and circles in the parched grass of the carpet,
the weave tough as granite, the floorboards tougher.
I pick him up and head for the door.
He can tour the dry moon of the back porch.

          2

Sun flies off a thousand puddles.
From the bedroom window I see corpses covering streets
and sidewalks. They are like limp twigs,
each aimed at dry spots distant as planets.
Inside, my houseguest is gone, over the threshold
or bound for the basement through some chink
in the rug's woof and warp.
                    By noon
the neighborhood is clear, dregs taken up by starlings,
the last of the dead black and dry
as ruined shoes. Water bleeds off into the canyons
and draws, sun gnaws into the garden.
And deep below, the worms begin to rise, ascending
like steam. When I am quiet, I hear them
between drops from eaves and trees.
I hear their soft hiss sifting upward
through the half-moist earth, a dream of dust.

HEART ATTACK

Throwing his small, blond son
into the air, he begins to feel it,
a slow-motion quivering, some part
broken loose and throbbing with its own pulse,
like the cock's involuntary leaping
toward whatever shadow looms in front.

It is below his left shoulder blade,
a blip regular as radar, and he thinks of wings
and flight, his son's straight soar and fall
out of and into his high-held hands.
He is amused by the quick change
on the boy's little face: from the joy

of release and catch, to the near terror
at apex. It is the same with every throw.
And every throw comes without
his knowing. Nor his son's. Again
and again, the rise and fall, like breathing,
again the joy and fear, squeal and laughter,

until the world becomes a swarm of shapes
around him, and his arms
go leaden and prickled, and he knows
the sound is no longer laughter
but wheezing, knows he holds his son
in his arms and has not let him fly

upward for many long moments now.
He is on his knees, as his son stands,
supporting him, the look on the child's face
something the man has seen before:

not fear, not joy, not even misunderstanding,
but the quick knowledge sons

must come to, at some age
when everything else is put aside—
the knowledge of death, the stench
of mortality—that fraction of an instant
even a child can know, when
his father does not mean to leave, but goes.

TERMITES

In one great spasm under the sun
the porch swallows you to the waist.
You stand there, sunk in a mire
of footsteps and disbelief,
blinking, as though you'd been
betrayed by an old friend.
Dust of the half-dry rot floats damply
around you, smelling of roots
and cool soil, mixes with the wind
and is gone.
          For an instant
you take your short fall for a mineshaft,
the headlong plummet of a heart attack.
Then all your family look on,
crouched on threshold
or peering through bannisters at ground level.
Before their sigh of relief, before
their laughter, and yours,
you see yourself a patient, a prisoner,
a dying man surrounded by doctors,
the hanged man.
          And you see more:
the intricate combs of the termites,
a trough worn by years of passage
before and behind the door. You kneel
and look closer. The whole underside
of the porch is a perfect mosaic of paths
and wrinkles, the wood's great mark of age.
When your head sinks out of sight,
you can almost hear your family begin to call,
some standing back, others inching out
very close to where you had been.

THE SECRET LIFE IN EVERY STANDING THING

1

It is the secret life in every standing thing,
every live and dead unmoving man
or piano, every car or truck, every wall
and roof and zinging trash can lid.

Vinegar Joe awoke above his restaurant. Downstairs
the water glasses rang like chimes, wine
goblets sang from their clear, immaculate throats.
Joe sat upright, and the bed lurched.

There was a calling in the world, a roar,
a shriek, a growl, a whisper. It was a howl,
a baying. It was lamentations, madness,
all things falling, falling toward the empty center.

The screen pocked outward, instantly gone.
Curtains sucked away, slick as linguini. In a second
Joe was uncovered, his lone sheet
flapping over the room like a lame bird.

Chill came through his bones, all
the hair on his body rose up prickling.
His teeth hammered, and the bed flung
up and dumped him out, the mattress

quick through a window half its size.
Joe skidded over the floor, the close nap
of the carpet burning his fingertips,
the bed frame sunk in the plaster wall.

The springs across the opening sang ululations
to the dead, and Vinegar Joe wept to be there,

hanging in his room by a hand on the radiator pipe
and another knotted in the wobbling coils.

He could see it all, all down the breathing street.
He could not look away, his face mashed against
a circle of springs, his eye that would not close
before the horror. He believed he saw the face of a god.

2

It was the springs that spoke to him, the springs
that saved him. It was the shape of them,
like the storm itself, an infinite coil
of air and debris, a spinning call of curse and prayer.

The cloud came straight for him.
Like a child's top, it grazed the walls
on each side of the street and ricocheted out.
In the building opposite, every floor

collapsed, and Joe saw there was no dust.
All things lighter than the earth were inhaled.
No smoke, no rain, no splinters.
Windows dissolved in a vapor. Joe saw

cars jettisoned, speeding more surely,
accelerating more quickly than their owners ever dreamed.
Parking meters screwed down and exploded
or sank box-deep in the sidewalks.

The restaurant sign rose up before his window,
floating free of the building, yet still aglow
with some miraculous neon. The night was alive
with three dozen tablecloths of gingham.

3

Then there was rain and thunder, the springs
swung away from the window,
and he fell back into his room, still now
but pitching in his tight-spun eyes.

Above him the bed frame hung on the wall,
and the window behind it crashed and flickered.
Lightning lit the room and the world.
A half-moon cut curled from his jaw to his left eye.

Fires came. Natural gas returned
to its severed pipes and ignited, the counting
of the bodies began, and Joe criss-crossed
his neighborhood. A block away was untouched.

Now night was woven with its human noises,
sirens and bullhorns, rev and grunt
of backhoe and crane, all the man-made alarms
and implements of hope, insubstantial and frail.

Vinegar Joe sat in his restaurant, behind
the wheel of a '59 Ford. He found a tablecloth,
folded it double, and spread it on the dash.
He found a wine goblet with only a chipped base

and three bottles of chianti balanced on a slanted shelf,
all cleanly uncorked. He crossed the wires
of the starter switch, tuned in music on the radio,
and waited for the light of morning.

It was what he believed he could do.
Then, idly, his half-empty goblet held

on the curve of the steering wheel,
he began tracing the moist crystal edge.

A column of music, a constant note
from deep in the breath-blown throat of the goblet,
and the hair on Joe's body came up electric.
The car radio joined in, and the night

was clotted with an otherworldly singing,
sirens and diesel bawlings blocked out.
Beneath him, Joe felt the seat of the Ford
awaken, a fluttery, spun-wire warbling that throbbed

in the cut on his face, the half-moon scored down
his temple and cheek, as though it held there
some invisible, crystalline shell, in which
he could hear an ocean of breathing.

THE BELIEFS OF A HORSE

In the field out back
there are some sheep, fat
and unsheared; two heifers;
and a pinto horse, his spots
like a map of continental drift.
One day soon a man will come
with his pistol and his high-backed
truck and take away the sheep
and the heifers, leaving
around the gate the steaming piles
of viscera, blood gathering
at the low point in a slow
and thickening rivulet.
The fence rails will fill up
with ravens. The air will throb
with bluebottle flies.
While all this time the horse
will merely stand, waiting for his
day on the trail,
as still as he can, monumental,
barely breathing, believing
among the flickers of leaves,
the slow-passing cloud shadows,
that he is lost
on the earth's great sea, that he is an island
on which the breeze quietly laps
and the sun passes by in its current,
the fence a near horizon
that will someday break wide with sails.

LOVER OF FIRE

1

Musk-wet, hay smells, the acrid sweet
aroma of horse dung. It is night.
The watchman one time at ten o'clock passes
then slouches in his office under the grandstand
and sleeps. He keeps his radio on
the all-night talk and squabble show
from St. Louis. When his phone rings,
the caller must believe no one could sleep
through such caterwauls and hollers.

Now I scale the fence, chain link
and well above my head, the last foot
strung aslant with barbed wire,
dropping as I have these twenty nights
to move among the stables like a spirit,
a presence almost acknowledged
by the low nickers here, a head-thrown snort
or snuffle there, and everywhere the breathing,
huge and dark, hot and damply sexual.

I come to them as a dream.
My hand on their flanks calls forth
a twitch—quick, insignificant, powerful.
Imagine so much precision
within your flesh, like a mountain
aware of a sliver of stone,
the night sky winking its feeblest star
across a billion to this place. All night
I watch to make out its whisper: it is *fire.*

2

Hay transcends itself. From my lighter
it leaps and stretches, bright
as the jockeys' silks, all the empty end
stalls quickly glaring. Already in
the low shining, the step-clop and whinnying,
I know the terror unrolls with the smoke.
One by one they begin wrenching,
eye whites flashing in the flame light,
kicking horror-driven at the hard stall doors.

Outside among the trailers I am hidden.
The watchman runs past, his keys
ringing like parade regalia. He is saying
to the stars "Oh Jesus God
Oh Jesus God . . . " And inside, the horses
are wild, the supple necks twisting,
pampered hoofs clattering the gray
unyielding wood: the many stallions,
the colts, the ghostly dreams of mares.

VOLUNTEERS

Siren over snow, blare
and howl of it over the year's
worst blizzard. I am up
crashing into clothes
and furniture, still
tugging on my gloves as I run
and slog the single snow-clogged block
to where the night glows gold.

It is the community center,
poor old false-fronted, hollow-toned
hall, now ablaze at eaves
and ridge pole, burning
from the top down, like a candle
or a flare, a campfire
planted in the pit
of winter night.
Del Heywood kicks in the front door,
calls for help. "Let's
get the snooker table, boys!"
A few of us gather near
the entrance. Even in the winter
chill the heat is fierce, the fire
now drawing through the open door,
exploding through the roof tins,
turning for one long moment
this blizzard to a snow of sparks.

Del peers in, up
at the rafters filigreed
in flames, and we all walk
back across the street
to stand among the gathering crowd

in front of the Rexall,
in the lee of the wind,
in a silence like none of us
has ever heard.

We let her go that night.
Old hall of silly dances,
bingo parlor, scene of every
meeting no one remembers so well
as where, now that the new
school is in, with a gym
and a theater, many clean
linoleumed classrooms,
and a flat roof already sagging.
By the time the false front falls,
everyone adult who could heave
through two feet of snow
is huddled at the curb
across the street, volunteers
in this cold and snowy place, warming
to the fall of ancient timbers,
gold on every quiet face.

MOWING

Sleepy and suburban at dusk,
I learn again the yard's
geometry, edging around the garden
and the weedy knots of flowers, circling
trees and shrubs, giving
a wide berth to the berry patch,
heavy and sprawled out of its bounds.
Shoving such a machine
around a fairway of dandelions,
it is easy to feel absurd.
The average lawn, left alone
one hundred years, could become
a hardwood forest. An admirable project.
Still I carry on, following week on week
the same mowing pattern, cutting edges,
almost sprinting the last narrow swaths.
And tonight, as I mow over
the bushels of fallen peaches,
sending pits soaring over the neighbors' fences,
seems hardly any different.
But on one crooked march I walk
across the thin hidden hole
to a yellowjacket hive. The blade pulls
them up from their deep sweet chamber
just as my bare legs go by.

A bee lands heavily,
all blunder and revenge, and the sting
is a quick embrace and release,
like the dared kid's run and touch
of a blind man. I'm blind now
with the shock and pain of it,
howling in a sprint toward the house,

the mower flopped on its side, wild blade loose
in the darkening air.
                    Later,
the motor sputtered quiet, starved by tilt,
I'm back in the twilight,
a half-dozen stings packed in wet tobacco,
carrying a can of gasoline, a five-foot torch.
The destruction is easy: shove can
slow to entranceway lip, pull
back and light torch, use torch
to tip can. One low *whump* and it's over.
A few flaming drones flutter out and fall.
Stragglers, late returners, cruise
wide circles around the ruins.
In the cool September night they fly
or die. In the morning I finish my chores.

All the way to winter the blackened hole
remains. On Christmas Eve a light
late snow covers it and all
the lawn's other imperfections: crabgrass
hummocks, high maple roots,
the mushroom-laden fairy ring that defies
obliteration and appears every spring
more visible than ever. Standing
in the window, the scent
of pine powerful around me,
the snap of wood undoing itself in the stove,
I wonder at this thin and cold
camouflage, falling,
gradually falling over what has gone
and grown before. And I hear
that other rattle and report, that engine

driven by another fire. I think of a gold
that is sweet and unguent, a gold
that is a blaze of years behind me.
I hear wind in its regular passes
blowing across the roof,
feel in my legs a minute and icy tingling,
as though I have stood too long
in one place or made again another wrong step,
as though the present itself
were a kind of memory, coiled, waiting,
dying to be seen from tomorrow.

YARD WORK

I am seven years old
when a neighborhood maniac kills my dog
with a pitchfork. It is mid-
May. My father and I carry the corpse
in a red wagon, wrap it in
a bedspread, and bury it deep
in the backyard.
                                    All summer long
with a number 2 shovel my father nips
at that tilted yard, and I dream at night
he struggles with its grassy edge, to lift it
and snap it like a mussed blanket.
In the morning, though, there is only the regular
chink and *slop* of his hopeless shovel.

I dream he must do this. I dream
he is digging the maniac's monstrous grave,
that he will slit that fat man's belly
with the tines of his own pitchfork.

One day, after school begins, I come over the hill
to see the yard sodded and level
as slow-rising water, a neat white cross
on the dog's grave. My father sits
on his heels, cradling his shovel
like a dangerous weapon, sipping lemonade
from a metal canteen.
                                    I have never seen
anyone so tired. And if he smiled through
his dusty face then, I've forgotten.
He said over his shoulder nothing special,
but walked to the house stooped and sore,
loaded with the freight of a good man.

PART TWO

We are the bees of the invisible. We frantically plunder the visible
of its honey, to accumulate it in the great golden hive of the invisible.

—Rilke

FIREFLIES

Now there are no fireflies. Once
there were, and we caught them,
our white sweaters glinting
in the dusk, chasing after children.
They were like that, like children
or the very old, doddering in slow flight.
We'd charge any flash and wait
at arm's length for another. And always,
there was. Once we kept them
in an unwashed honey jar, two dozen
snagged and flickering on the oozy sides.
Carefully we plucked them away and wrote
with the smears of their phosphorescence
our names on a stone wall,
then afterwards licked our fingers,
and they were sweet and golden.

for Hugh Nichols

The man believes in blood, in the dog
beside him so remarkably alive, keen
in his eyes and up-pricked ears,
miraculously not bolting, loosed
from the long year's chain-link kennel.
He believes in blood, in his heart
drumming like a grouse, the dog
out front still as earth and holding,
blood in them all holding, still
as the dog is still, the man,
the birds.
    We might leave them
as they are now, frozen
in the thistle-cluttered gully,
below wheat stubble, the noisy arcs
of grasshoppers like a cartoon model
of the cosmos. It could be a painting,
fall gold and salmon sky at dawn,
framed and lit from above,
mounted in the den
by the blue-black steel and sweet oil
redolence of the gun rack. But how
account for the blood, then,
knowing in this scene it is not posed
but poised, that it must, before we go,
resume its motions inevitable as sun-
light or stars.
    Four birds flush,
one falls, and the gun shatter tumbles
over the valley like a stone,
like the sound a star might make
in its plummet, or the thistle,
wind-blown, to the smallest,

most sensitive ears. The dog
cavorts, retrieves, his soft mouth
innocent. A smear of blood
crosses the man's hand and jacket,
a brush stroke he understands.

THE SKULL OF A SNOWSHOE HARE

I found it in the woods, moss-mottled,
hung at the jaws by a filament
of leathery flesh. We have painted it
with Chlorox, bleached it
in that chemical sun, boiled loose
the last tatters of tissue,
and made of it an heirloom,
a trophy, a thing that lasts, death's
little emissary to an eight-year-old boy.

What should it mean to us now
in its moon-white vigil on the desk?
Light from the hallway makes it loom
puffball brilliant, and I look.
For no good reason but longing
I am here in your room,
straightening the covers, moving a toy,
and lightly stroking your head,
those actions I have learned to live by.

If we relish the artifacts of death,
it's for a sign that life goes on
without us. On the mountain snows
we've seen the hare's limited hieroglyphics,
his signature again and again
where we've skied. And surely
he has paused at our long tracks there,
huddled still as moonlight, and tested
for our scents long vanished in that air.

We live and die in what we have left.
For all the moon glow of that bone
no bigger than your fist, there is more

light in the way I touch you
when you're sleeping: the little electric sparks
your woolen blankets make together,
the shape of your head clear
to my hand in the half-light,
and this page, white as my bones, and alive.

Arrayed on the kitchen table,
the shells, salt and freshwater, simple
and ornate; starfishes, tiny and dry.
There are the teeth of deer and elk,
the long tail feathers of a pheasant;
skulls of rodent and bird, shell
of turtle, the eye-domes of opercula,
those unhinged stop-gaps from under seas.
Antlers, snake rattles, the glossy claw

of an owl, still honed and gleaming.
And the bones beyond counting—horse,
fox, gopher, goat. Now you and I
take note, do what all collectors do
from time to time: we look,
inventory by hand and eye,
and lean back pleased by our possessions,
so dubious, useless, and prized.
Strung out here in ranks, in piles

and rib-curved chevrons, it is
a museum of life and death, little boy.
Take the tiny crab from the beach
near Tacoma. You asked once about its life,
about a loneliness and isolation
I could see on your face that you
yourself have felt. In its padded cell,
its plastic sarcophagus, it sidles on,
brittle as rime ice, tenuous as leaves.

No, none of it will live again,
not one dazzling feather or bone,
not the crab or the unbrained, unbodied

skull of the mouse. And, finally,
nothing we have amassed here
has any currency we can live by in this world,
though it is a place hard
bent on destruction, deep in death.
No one will ever steal these jewels.

Still, by this plenitude we are known,
if only to ourselves and your small pals,
now gathered round the table,
awestruck, dumb, and beginning already to itch
with a sourceless, ineffable envy.
Four years old, six, and seven,
the three of you stand at the table like pilgrims
in the door of a holy mosque,
like kittens at the threshold

of a blurry, undreamed-of world.
Then you begin, each one of you, lifting
and looking, delicately holding, touched
in some clear way for the first time
by death. From each small hand
to the other passes the graceful salmon spine.
A few long ribs are still intact,
though the bony pivots are frozen in place.
It passes up the line, rising

from four-year-old, to six, then seven,
upright, aimed as it had been
a year or more before, upstream,
out through time's sweet conduit, a river,
bound for the stream of its birth.

Your hands flesh it out. It fins hard
through rapids and years, and I
can see on your faces—quiet, clear—
how the flesh still works, and you believe.

TOUCHING THE CARP

They looked reptilian in the lake's mud
edges, and we knew there were some who ate
the bony flesh. We meant only to touch
them, the heavily cross-hatched backs and sides,
the blue and silver bellies upturned
in the half-gone light at Rend Lake.

I wonder now if we ever meant to fish the lake,
a prairie reservoir dense with weeds and mud.
Her father came to the window when I turned
in his driveway at eight
o'clock that morning. The rusty sides
of my old car had not seen the touch

of sponge or chamois in years. But touch
was all our aim, and Rend Lake,
any lake, would do—its dark side
roads, its impassable mud
that kept away the crowds. We had eight
long hours of love ahead, I had just turned

seventeen, and she turned
to kiss me just outside the straining touch
of her father's field of vision. We kissed, we ate
lunch, we baited and fished the lakes
of ourselves, played in the sweet, salt mud
flesh is at seventeen, in the back seat, side by side.

Just before we left, we walked the near side
of Rend Lake, held our clammy hands, and turned
to see them: in swirls of mud
and water, sodden shore grasses, a mass of carp touched

together, boiling at the lake's
shallow edge, a roiling sculpture of eight

or a dozen. There were some who ate
them, but we only knelt alongside
those trash fish, so lovely in the drab lake
debris, so graceful in their weaving turns,
so intricately coiled and lightly touching:
we meant to touch them as we knelt in that mud.

And all eight or ten or more, at their slow turns
sidelong in the shallows, were lovingly touched and touched,
then swam for the lake, leaving trails of amber mud.

THOSE RICHES

The week after your father left
you still carried his note in your wallet,
and on the night before the bank
said they'd come for the car,
we were on our way to St. Louis,
our last dime in the gas tank, and you
every way you could find
abusing that sad family sedan,
pounding the dash for the radio it lacked,
shifting without the clutch
and wringing from its feeble six
every stinking, oil-ridden mile per hour.
Down the long hill past the Catholic cemetery,
under the dead viaduct
and into the bottom lands we rolled.
You spoke of jobs you might have soon
at this or that plant or refinery,
smoked my cigarettes, thought
you'd save up for a car and a tattoo.
Through the banks of smog,
the swampland haze, great flames rose
above the foundries and steel mills,
and there was nothing in school
so bright. It was Saturday night,
and you would never go back, not ever.

We found our way to Gaslight Square
and drove slowly down its streets.
You refused to acknowledge the sidewalk crowds,
the soul and blues, the smack jazz
seething from the nightclubs.
At the last bright reaches we were stalled
by traffic, and a whore in hot pants

called from a Laundromat doorway. Sugar,
she sang, and came outward. She walked
to your window, leaned her breasts on your arm,
grinned, and you turned and spat in her face.

What you could not accomplish that night
a handful of outraged, high-heeled prostitutes could.
They kicked at our fenders, spit
with amazing accuracy through our windows.
And with what you claimed to have seen and known
as a blackjack, one leering redhead
bashed in the windshield, turning all
its clear expanse to a sagging honeycomb
of safety glass, before the traffic opened
and we were on our way half blind
into the diesel-scented city night.

Could that have been what we were after,
that joy, those riches
reeling from destruction?
Ten blocks farther on we stopped
and forced the whole window out, down
onto the dash and floor and front seat,
then drove home with the summer highway
wind in our faces, laughing,
sitting in a gravel of glass
that flashed under streetlights,
in the full of the moon, like a carload of diamonds.

TORCH SONGS

I would speak of that grief
perfected by the saxophone, the slow
muted trombone, the low unforgettable cornet.
Theirs were the paths we followed
into the sexual forest, the witch's spellbound cabin,
the national anthems of longing.

Rhythm is the plod of the human heart,
that aimless walker down deserted streets
at midnight, where a tavern's neon keeps the pulse.
A horn man licks the blood
in tow, heavy and smooth,
and a song is in the veins like whiskey.

Does it matter then that men have written
the heartbreaks women make hurt?
that Holiday and Smith sang for one
but to the other? Or is everything equal
in the testimonies of power and loss?
Is the writer the body, the singer the soul?

Now your eyes are closed,
your head leaned back and off to one side.
Living is a slow dance you know
you're dreaming, but the chill at your neck
is real, the soft, slow breathing
of someone you will always love.

STAR DUST

That crooning they swooned for, all the moons in June
and sweet talk of broken hearts forever: the man
in his apartment hears buses hiss and roar
below his window, a television set next door,
but listens to Dorsey and Sinatra on the phonograph,
feels a quiet settle over his flesh, the laugh
of muted trumpets coming down soft as rain.

He could look for hours into the room's
empty spaces—the blind stares, his father called them.
And he knows it is melancholy, a nameless
yearning not for his own youth, but for that famous
eon of his father's, a blind time
before one war or another, and all those fine
fine tunes that lull him now to dream

without sleep. He believes a song
is a dream, memory nothing but a long
lyric he'll never completely know.
He thinks of his parents, years ago,
huddled on the old Ford's hood, wrapped
in a woolen blanket and watching the lake water lap
the shore under star shine. On the radio a song

from Dorsey and Sinatra rang the perfect omen.
Tonight is what they could not know, when
he would ache with his nothing, grow still
below the weight of what is empty, all that any song will
do. Like the star beaming outward past its death,
the buses and the rain he loses track of,
the music comes and goes, and he remembers again.

THE SOUND BARRIER

1

We were in our beds or daydreaming
out a window in school,
or we were simply running, the fleet
childish joy of motion through a still, dusty field.
It was silence that shattered.

In 1961 I was dreaming baseball
when the bomb of air blew up. The bed
lurched, I raised my head to hear the windows
clattering in their frames, my mother's trinkets ringing.
And when I settled back into sleep, the room fell away.
There was a rush of dreams like stars,
the rustle of bedclothes trailing off.

2

At the end of its road in Illinois
my father's house sat cracking in the cold.
A light from the kitchen window shone
a rectangle in the snow, my father
at the table yawning toward work.
The sweep of his hair left a mark on the window.
He leaned to see. A high flash
crossed the sky, the brief faded wash of its roar.

This is for you in that airplane, the exhilaration
you must have felt, my father cursing you
for everyone on earth.

THE GLOW

1

Above the playground, from the hung-out
highest limb of a creaking, leafless elm,
the bee hive breathed all summer long,
a low sizzle high up. It grew
like the mound of mud thrown out
by a crawdad, hurled up
on wind around the thick and empty limb,
a great bronze breast hung sweet
above the faces of children.

The sky was its own
electric fence. Every high and wobbly
fly ball fell from its arc
as though swatted down, an egg shoved off
the sky's blue table. And birds
gave the whole tree a berth,
even the woodpecker, who strayed
from his place among locusts
to patter a while the elm's infested trunk

and flew away wild in swoops
from the dark swarm
the hive hauled out to halt him.
Only the wind moved high in timber,
its hiss across leaves
a harmony to the bee's wiry buzzing.
Still they sent out sentries,
who fought the wind's tug and toss
and wound up lost, stung

out from sinking their skewers
all across an enemy's invisible flank.
On such days, the hive heaving

overhead, teachers called
in their students, and from the windows
all afternoon small gazes flared
hard, wondering if this day would be
the last of the bees' lording over,
the high hold held finally in check.

    2

Windows razzed with grit
and the great bowl of the playground
lay below the school, overflowing
with dust. All around
darkened to storm, and teachers
reviewed the choreographies
of disaster. Then came rain,
whipped in the sky to froth,
spattering onto glass its

million small scars. Here
and there a pane gave out
and the school sucked hard the cold
air. Halls filled with
files of frightened children,
rambling lunchless to the deep
and quiet cafeteria, some dazzled
silent, others sobbing, whimpering
for father, mother, sunshine.

They sat below the storm's
unmuffled engine, and when the walls
around them held they began
to laugh. The room roared
with the voices of children, voices

thrown high and excited by the wind
and their own clattering hearts.
Among such laughter and the scoots of stools,
every child forgot about the bees.

    3

Every one but the one who lived
next door, whose whole summer was spent
lolling in the cool near woods
and the playground's dusty spaciousness,
who daily gauged by his upheld thumb
the hive's expansion,
whose bedroom window caught every morning
the first early dronings.
This one hid among coats and sweaters

and the day's hollow clang
of lunch pails. Knowing
he had only until the rolls
were taken, he slipped out soon behind
his classmates, dodging teachers
in their last-minute swings, and walked
out into rain and chaos, the wind
aswirl with water and leaves,
with mud and birds and everything

but bees. With his left shoulder
he leaned downhill into the playground,
the school behind him paling to a hulk,
a shadow, before it was completely gone.
He looked down around him
for the minor landmarks a child
remembers, having studied this land

more carefully than any
textbook. But old grasses

swooned with the weight of weather.
There was nowhere a sign
he could sight from, no hummock of weed
that tripped him one day, no bare
mark of mud where second base
or third had received his slide.
Now the slant of the land itself
seemed wrong, and he sat
in the thunder and rain, and waited.

4

Among the stone rumbles of the storm,
wind yelping through trees and brush,
he heard the first low pop of the trunk
giving way, a wooden spoon
broken under water. The soft
mush of old heartwood sputtered,
quiet cardboard crackling, and then,
while the sparse crown swung silent
in its fall, there were only the sounds of storm.

It appeared black above him,
a wooden claw holding a hunk
of honey, workers, and wax.
He could hear the hive's
respiration, a million wings worrying
close and pungent air. Down
like some prehistoric bird it came,
from a Saturday movie and nightmare,
and he covered his face with his arms,

waited for the yank or crush.
But he was suddenly swaddled in tree.
All around him leaves and branches
closed in, nipping light and sharp his face
and arms, sending him a foot
in the air on the trunk's concussion,
and dumping at his feet, on his feet,
an offering of honey and comb,
gold and pearl all across him.

To his left he saw the ground a mass
of bees imbedded in their lives,
lifting up dizzy toward their deaths.
He saw against wet bark the queen
sealed in a dollop, still and perfect
as an amulet. A few drones grazed
his anointed body, as though
he were a large and bounteous flower.
He rose and walked into the rain.

        5

For a long while he wandered lost,
until the school rose up before him.
He walked through the door and passed
down halls littered with glass
and papers, slowly,
his feet clinging in their golden boots,
and descended the stairs
to be once again among the others,
children, teachers, who only then
noticed his absence and turned
to the door, uttered one low cry,
and stopped. The eyes

of every adult and child
turned to the figure in the doorway,
his clothes frayed, heavy with rain,
his face a smear of small bleeding cuts
and drops of honey, winking
in the lights like iridescent scabs.

From his shoes amber puddles flowed
outward. All up and down
his legs was a fresco of bees,
mementos, souvenirs
fastened to a plaque and varnished.
The room lay before him
like a photograph, every face caught
in the moment's quick shutter.
He will remember them that way,

frozen in their stares,
peering up at the miracle of him,
not knowing whether
the look in his eyes
was terror or the transfix
of high wind and venom. He will remember
himself in their eyes, the look
that will not go away
for years and years

of his life as someone partly other
than human, removed, as necessary
and dangerous as a bee,
as chosen and blessed as any survivor.
In the halls and on the playground,
on the streets, he will feel the glow of gold

they have seen around him, hear the whirr
they heard that day, as bees
came to life in his matted hair.

PART THREE

Speak out the wish like music, that has within it
The horn, the string, the drum pitched deep as grief.

—Louise Bogan

A PHOTO OF IMMIGRANTS, 1903

You could cry at their faces.
Father forces a smile
and Mother looks into the lens
as she must have looked for weeks
into the distances of the Atlantic.
The infant dangles her feet
against sack cloth, and the boy,
four maybe, looks up at his hand
in his father's, as though surprised
to find it there. Or perhaps
the look on his face is pain, his father
holding on too hard. The ship in back
loads for the return to Danzig:
crates of pencils, pistons, bolts of linen.
By its first moorage, these four will be on their way
to Cleveland or Chicago. They will have seen
the Statue of Liberty and looked past it
for the world. They will have sweltered
on the train all through Ohio
and August.
                    And in five years
they will write to their friends in Cracow,
enclose a few dollars, a new and cheerful photograph.
Father will tell in his most earnest prose
the ordeal of the Atlantic passage
and the ecstacy of arrival.
He will have himself removing his hat
and blowing kisses to the city, laughing
and clapping with his fellows. And that night
he will mail his letter, walking slowly
to the post office with his daughter.
He will hear two men there speak again
of the great lake to the north of the city

and vow to visit it when there is time.
He will stop and tell his daughter of his plans.
She will nod and walk on, walking oddly
on the sides of her feet, hoping
he will soon let go of her hand,
speak English, or loosen
at least his fierce and powerful grip.

THE CRÈCHE

It survived the loud, jostling train
from Baden to Berlin, and the heave
and slant, the pitch, pivot and lean
of the bad boat to New York.
She held it to her in a hatbox
stuffed with husks, all across steerage
and Pennsylvania, down the slow road
of the Ohio River to Cairo
and up the dirt tracks and coal-
paved paths to Frankfort, Illinois,
her sudden husband, her life.
She was mined for the children
in her, one daughter, then another,
a short seam, quick to clay,
and not a single son to save them.

But each December found her unfolding
from their sheaths the pale
figures from Dresden: Holy Mother, mild
worker in wood, stock reclined
and ruminant, the infant peering skyward
through His upheld hands. And through the years
we have come to know this story,
how starved, buried on scrip to the company store,
the miner came coal-hearted home,
winter just begun, his daughters already asleep,
and the crèche below a sprig of pine.
How blind in the peripheral light, unhelmeted
to rage, he crushed the manger and the tiny Lord
in his blackened right hand,
spat the word *woman* in her face,
and left that night and never returned.

There the story ends, but for one daughter
who married, bore another, who bore
a son, who fathered three boys—two that survived—
and one that passed on the crèche,
the Holy Mother, husband, endlessly
sleepy stock, and the gap since then gathered round,
its eloquent absence,
its grip more powerful than any man's.

Appalonea Miller Voisin (1840–1901)

There may have been a time when
your name went unnoticed: Amethyst,
Hortensia, and Emerald Maisie Hopes
were your chums, your names
sparkling off the page like so much paste
and silver plate. The Chinese
say you are not truly dead
until the last soul who knew your name
forgets it. Somehow we misplaced yours
against remarkable odds: a name
like a bird that sings its own,

or conjures up music
and hard fruit. Winesap, Golden
Delicious, the loud applause of wind
in the dry leaves of autumn.
But not a single shining image
of the human face. Grandfather's
grandmother, anyone we both knew
is dead now, and rooting
through certificates and microfilm
we've found every vital statistic but your face.

So I talk, and your name
is the only answer. Appalonea. Apotheosis
of appellations, a plum of pure sound.
Apollo, Apollonius, Apollinaire.
The great Johnny Appleseed
who gave us a peachy cider, a press,
and a pint of apple jack. I'm drunk
in the swirl of your name, the way
it applies to everything I see:

that strong grayish horse
across the field: Appaloosa,
a portrait but not a picture,
a prize, a poem, Appalonea.

WEAVER OF WIND

Her hands go on in the dark,
tatting doilies over quilts
and blankets, patient arabesques
of sleep and fine string.
She follows a pattern
borrowed from a garden spider.

In the morning she remembers
blindness, come closer
with every hook of her needle,
the shuttle's each loud pass.
Her world moves in a milky blur.

She remembers too the last months
and what they have taken from her:
the loom, the sewing machine
with its sweet creaky treadle,
all her needles.

Now she sits in her chair
on the front porch, knotting
and unknotting the wind,
tying in labyrinthine bows
the strings of her apron, braiding
her hair to a sleek, white rope.

And after work her children come
to do their unraveling, to help
with her dinner. They hurry
along with their knives
and hot plates, fret over
the clock and the dust on the furniture.
They do all they believe they can.

They kiss lightly the top of her head
and leave her washing vegetables,
not noticing the sift of her hands
through lacey carrot tops,
her fingers swirling in the colander,
tracing stars.

RUNNING IN YOUR SLEEP

You're running, not
the breathy strides
of a woman from her
body's relentless spreading,
but running for your life
out of dream that lopes
over years like low hurdles.
Among the breweries
and workers' bars, the dark
stadium, the loading docks
thundering across the highway
below you, you're running
out of a past as quick as it is
brutal, relentless as tomorrow
and the treadmill you sleep on,
the sad race every night
has come to be.
               Of him
you remember only his small,
thick frame, his glasses,
the wheeze of his chase
that sounded every breath
like his last. You remember him
gaining. You were young then.
Today you'd never keep up
his pace, but that night
he kept on, and so did you,
dropping first your purse
then your long, worn coat
as obstacles along the causeway,
tripping him up in the darkness
and making him angry.
It was his shouting that caused

your crying, your calling
to your mother, who
for all the time she could not afford
for love held you long until light
and long nights after.

Now you read how safe it is
to be frightened, and you are.
No one ever chased me
with death on his hands, rape,
choking desperate and refusing to go
down. No one saw me
working beyond my age, gave me
ruin as a legacy, hope as a cause
already lost.
                     Running as you will
until memory gives out,
there's little help a son can offer.
Only this: all breath gets stirred
in the lungs. The cry of a baby
can lapse into the softest sleep,
the rasps of lovers
sometimes go on and on.
And lovers will lose their easy motions
when they pass mirrors, when
they see in regrettable lights
the long, long ways they've come,
frightened, sad, and lonely.
But some of them are still
caught up in each other,
running away from the spouse
we must all lie down with,
and toward the other,

those years and moments between,
the motions of the body
and the soul, running.

THE LEANING HOUSE

for my grandmother

Everything leans north
where wind splits
the corner of the house.
Storm nights, cellophane covers
on windows swell in and out,
shirts filled and emptied of breath.
Gravy, dumplings in their bowls,
milk and coffee in cups: each leaves
a tilted ellipse above the old table,
and every year another thin wedge of matchbook
slips under the south legs.
Behind us, bottles in the icebox pitch
back as though they would lean
out of reach, and we eat,
half of us straining past our laps
to our dishes, others drawing back
every bite with a push of the legs.
For the woman who lives here
the world is the uneven place, her home
as flat as a frozen lake. She walks
these halls and creaking rooms
with a balance blossomed in habit, leaning
between us one hot dish after another,
eyeing all our plates and smiling.
We eat, and keep holding on.

AUBADE FOR MOTHERS

1   The Ritual of Expulsion and Yearning

I am alone in the nursery corridor,
moving window to window,
perusing each child's melon face.
I see my own in her bassinet
of aluminum and glass, my own
faint in the finger-clouded pane.
The swell to my abdomen is gentler
today. There are spasms, intermittent,
expected, the ritual of expulsion and yearning.

The first memory is presence, first
sensation is loss. These are shapes,
colors, blood-muffle or chorus of winds.
In his swaddling before me, someone's
child flinches and feints, ducks
his wizened little face quick
behind his hands. What figures
can he see in his dreams? what terrors?
what sanctuaries of flesh and bone?

The nurses have cuffed my daughter's hands,
the slash of her newborn nails.
But for now she sleeps peacefully, open-mouthed,
lightly drooling. When I lean away
from the window, I see her
through the mark my forehead has left,
a fog of my own making,
through which she outwardly sails
on the certain and ritual waves.

2   A Cloth of Reunion and Love

Now they are all asleep, my friends
and their children, my sons, my daughter
and my husband, weary of so much elation.
I have waited for this instant. I came back
to the living room, banked the fire,
and began to sit, to stare
out at the common air of all our lives,
the night our breaths have woven
into fabric, a cloth of reunion and love.

The air breathed out by beloved sleepers
is like a dance of souls
or a system of weathers—storm clouds,
clear skies: I see now that the dew is no more
than an aura made plain every day,
the pure energy of children,
a fog of heat rising from the bed rolls.
How strange it is, a mother's breath
coming from one I knew as a child!

Her sleep sound is a soft wet rasp,
her daughter's just the same. Her son
rumbles like me: it will always be spring
in his life, short storms, wild greenings.
I listen to her breathing, my friend's,
and I am lulled. I should be
asleep too. But I can't sleep now.
I am a mother myself, there is tomorrow,
and now the night comes down with its rag.

3   Aubade for Mothers and Their Lives

The seconds screamed, the minutes writhed
toward midnight. But now the room
grows back its familiar objects,
the suck and wash of the respirator is less,
my mother's sad dying body still lives.
At their homes my brothers are
readying themselves for my call,
and I feel like dancing, like singing:
an aubade for mothers and their lives.

My joy is not strange: we are alone,
my mother and I. She cannot speak,
I won't. But I think to myself how
the tubes from her body dangle and rise
like *ivy*. It is a pun
she would be pleased by. Death
when it comes will be a man.
He will nod to me, deferential, and, waving,
Mother will leave this grave to the earth.

This morning, it is April, the crocuses glisten
dewy under the sun, the seasonal birds
babble. Something like my mother's
soul wavers in the air above her body.
Suddenly I know the moment
of my conception, a morning like this!
I long for my husband, cuffing the children
at home. And now I am laughing:
I think that I will never be alone.

THE OWL   *for Phyllis Wright*

I was young, and leaned
against the gray boards, almost sleeping.
Newly weaned from the drill and splash,
the chamber pot's porcelain contingency,
I knew just enough of darkness
and nightsounds, the musky aroma
of the outhouse, to doze there,
my nightdress gathered round me like a flourish.

When the owl lit, I knew it was God.
My first look from the door's
slim crack was proof: white
and blazing with moonlight, it lifted outward and made
in two great and silent wing flaps
the chicken house, dark and unclucking
across the yard. The black eyes rolled over
the lawn like searchlights.

Again and again it flew across
the still world, silent as a star.
Until once, as it left its perch above me,
it tilted and came instantly down
on my yearling gray cat. Just a flash
of talon, a gnarled leg of amber,
and both were gone, the winging silent as ever
across hayfields, the pulse of wings

a silver trail into trees. I ran inside
and shivered in my bed until daylight. Since
that day, I have wondered
how I came to be there, sleepy
and desperate in the stillness. The cat
likewise, yawning in its moonlight

meander after rodents and moths.
And the bird, the snowy owl,
winging effortless as breath.

Little girls rose then, and padded
out blinking, scratching, unafraid. And cats
have always been the denizens of farmscapes.
It is a world removed now
from my daughters, who still wander from their rooms,
sleepy and tidal, indoors, wakened by the moon.
I lie in my bed and listen, remembering.

Then I sleep, the dream taking me
away on great white wingbeats,
regular as moonrise, nightly as letting go.

MOON IN A MASON JAR

It was what you might as well wish for,
blue-in-the-face, pipe-dreamer.
Money taunts, another year
is gone by and still you're in that old coat,
those over-hauled dresses, your face
hand-tooled to a frown
while you dun by phone the other bad debtors.

Rue the day the fourth child was born,
rue worse the day it started.
Your hands are crabbed in wash water,
nails ravaged. And there is no sense
in happiness despite it all,
no glad release when, sweat-soaked,
you stack the last jar of fruit
on the pantry shelves and stand back to see them,
the yolky peaches, wine cherries,
the cool lunar lobes of the pears,
and the accompaniment each lid makes
as it pings and seals itself tight.

What My Father Believed

for my father & for my children

Logic and sermons never convince,
The damp of the night drives deeper into my soul.

—Whitman

AMERICAN MANHOOD

In the dull ache that is midnight for a boy
his age, I heard the sound of him first:
hiss of the pistol-grip hose from the garden
and the clatter a watery arc makes
coming down silver under streetlights,
on the day-warmed pavement of the road.
And though I muttered at first
to be awakened, I stand now in the window
upstairs, naked and alert, the cool breeze
sweet with the blossoms of locusts.

My wife murmurs, stirs. She is a slope of white
in the bedclothes, dunes of softness
below the light from the window
and the single blind eye of the clock.
"It's just Travis," I say, hoping
she'll lapse again into sleep.

I hope she'll sleep because he is a boy,
fourteen, soft yet himself, unwhiskered.
He believes he is the only one
awake, the only one alive in a world
of cruel nights and unbearable silence.
His parents snore, their house is dark.
He crouches on the curb
in just his pajama bottoms, barefoot,
swirling figure eights into the air trafficked
by insects and the fluttering, hunting bats.

Tonight he speaks a language I believe
I must have known, in the time before, those years
when a boy's body imagines the world, the heartbeat
rhythm of water on the road, the riches

coined by streetlights, the smell of the night
that is everything at once, alterable
and contained—all that keeps him awake
long after I've gone back to bed.

But before sleep comes, I listen, until the noise
he makes is my own even breathing, and I remember how
the old rented guitar I learned on smelled of music,
how the young married woman across the street
robbed me of the power of speech,
and how I wandered one night the alleys
of the town I grew up in, a brick in my hand,
breaking thermometers, taillights, and windows,
and went home and laughed aloud and wept.

NIGHT RISING

After an hour of fighting it, I pull
on my boots, leave my son sleeping
in the tent, and stand pissing in a darkness
absolute to my burning, sleep-swollen eyes.
In the last year this rising has become
common, a nightly battle of will and bodily want,
the fist and the clamped thighs, the dark.

A day of steady rain, fog in the bones,
bad fishing, has left me halfway through the night
sore from sleeping on the ground. I chill
as my bladder empties. From the great dying
cedars droplets fall on my bare back and arms,
the river murmurs in the distance.
Before I awakened, at the dim edge of urgency,
I dreamed my own father groaning in the night,
easing from the door of the station wagon
we slept in, the cool heft of night air
hitting me, the dome light momentarily on,
then off, on again, then off for good.

Now groggy with sleep, I can't recall
what is memory and what is dream.
If such a night ever happened—the minute
of solitary half-sleep, darkness tattooed
with the dome light's blue afterimages—
I can't say. Nor can I say for sure when I finish
which way I've come from the tent.

Without moon or stars or flashlight, I listen
behind the river for rain, the ping of it
on a left-out pot, drum on the pickup's hood.
I consider calling my son's name

but know how soundly the boy sleeps,
how the bellow it would take to wake him
would frighten him as well. So I move,
one slow step after another, my hands
swimming the black fog before me,
finding my way in time.

HIS FATHER'S WHISTLE

For hours the boy fought sleep,
strained against the whir of cicadas, moths
at the screens bumbling, night's
silver breezes, to hear out on the country road
his father's car rumbling in gravel.
He watched for the sweep of headlights
on the ceiling, a quick rush down
the driveway, then footsteps barely audible
over the lawn, his father's whistle.
Half a verse, a sliver of chorus, and his father was in
the house, quiet, the boy already drifting
in the night, asleep before the hand caressed his face.

It seemed to the boy that his life would be this way
forever, that out of the murmuring shadows,
the terror of distance, the danger of all
he did not know, there would come an order
like the one a melody imposed upon silence,
his father's whistle among night sounds,
as though breath, a song,
and a boy's simple fear of the dark,
were a man's only reasons for whistling.

ECONOMICS

He learned economics in the shade
of a truck, a flatbed owned by the man
he worked for, who owned as well the tons
of concrete on it, owned the farm never farmed
but mowed, the Ford dealership in town,
a great white house across the way, and a daughter
there with her friends, sunbathing by the pool.
A ton of cement in hundred-pound bags
he'd already stacked on pallets in the barn.
It was Saturday, after lunch, sun seared
his neck and shoulders, flickered
from the drops on the girls by the pool,
and shone in the suffocating dust
he saw through. Though his eyes were closed
when the kick hit his heels,
he wasn't sleeping. He was awake
and dreaming in the splashes and laughter,
resting in the dust and truck-smelling shade,
leaned against a gritty rear wheel.

And so it was the joy he imagined
tied then to the owner's sneer
and warning. Joy, and the rage he let build
through a ton-and-a-half of lifting
and lugging, the loathing for a man
who owned all the world he could see
from high on the back of a flatbed truck,
sweeping dust into the air
and watching when that man came out
to the pool, soft and flabby,
and grinned through an oafish cannonball
that made the girls laugh, applauding like seals.
It was a rage that cooked in his old

black car, that ground in its slow start,
and lunged like its badly slipping clutch.
He longed in his sweat for speed and oblivion,
the thrum of good tires, the deep-lunged roar
of power, a wheel in his hands
like a weapon, turn by premeditated turn.

"You best work, boy, or your whole life'll be
as shitty as today." When the kick had come
he flinched, involuntarily. His one knee rose,
his left arm blocked his face, and in the grit
of his right glove his fist closed on
the readiness to hit. He was ashamed
to be caught, ashamed for his flinch,
ashamed he could not, as the owner glared down
at his startled eyes, leap to his feet and murder him.
He was ashamed by his silence, by the ache
even then in his back and arms, the guilt
he could never disprove. The route home
that day derided him, maddeningly slow
through marginal farms and identical suburbs.
His mother's howdy-doo repulsed him,
and his father's little wink seemed the grimace
of a ninny. It was Saturday night,
he had no date, but didn't sleep until morning,
when he rose anyway, hating his face in the mirror.

Monday, washing as always the endless line
of new cars, he began to understand
the limitations of revenge: murder, fire,
the daughter's humiliation at school—
these were risks he couldn't take. Even scratches
here and there on the cars. He cursed his luck

and scrubbed, twisted the chamois so tightly
it tore, and Sven, the old one-armed Swede
he worked with, shook his head and sighed.
"You just wash, Hercules," he said. "I'll dry 'em."
So he went on, lathering and scrubbing,
quiet, Sven telling dirty jokes,
analyzing the bouquet, the savor of women,
offering his wisdom in every field
until the boy threw down his sponge, spit,
looked the old man deeply in the eye
and asked him in all his feeble goddam brilliance
what the hell was he doing here, washing cars
a half a buck a crack with a boy.

And when he saw Sven's expression
it almost came out, all the simple story
about sweat and mistakes, cement and rage
and the long ride to nowhere through a life
he couldn't stand. What would it have taken
for the shame to come out, the shame
now for hurting an old man, for kicking,
like any cool and flabby man who owned a world.
Instead the boy worked, behind him
Sven mopping up, silent until the last three sedans,
when he flipped the chamois on a hood and said,
"Here, goddam ye. I'm tired. You finish 'em."
And so he was alone at the end,
when the owner's daughter arrived, brown
and gut-hurtingly beautiful in a shiny new car.
She waved to him and smiled, Sven was gone,
his blood sped in his veins, and he knew
she'd come no nearer to him ever in his life.

FOR THE LAST SUMMER

That summer with a thousand Julys
nothing mattered but the sweat on a girl's chest,
the sun's crazy blue weather, and a young man's
hands electric with want. The wind
above convertibles sighed in the cottonwood leaves,
the stars were stars, and the moon ached
in its own silver heaven. He was king
of the swath a train whistle cut.

Crazy for speed, he held the girl and the wheel
and plummeted toward the bottomlands,
foundry lights ablaze in the distance,
and war let him sing the songs he swore
he'd never forget. That summer
of week-long nights, blossom-dark,
fragrant with dew and a dust
as fine as milled flour, he dreamed.

And his dreams were all glory and light,
line drives that never fell, his friends
his friends forever, and war
let him sleep until noon and wake
with the scent of his girl around him,
remembering the night before—
how he sang of a loss he couldn't imagine,
of broken hearts he could almost believe.

That summer with a thousand Julys
the sun going down each afternoon was more
beautiful than the day before, the factory smoke
vermilion and rust in its slant, and the night-
hawks like needles stitching the darkness down.

Nothing smelled as sweet as the gasoline
he pumped, nothing arced so cleanly
as the shop towels he tossed toward their baskets.

The world rode shotgun and reclined
on the seat of his car, lovely in the glow
from the dash lights, soft and warm.
and he knew what it meant to adore. War
let him dawdle there, virtuoso of the radio,
king of the push buttons, and all that played
for him, in the only hours of his life he ever knew
as his own, was music, music, music.

SINATRA

That skinny fuck-up, all recklessness and bones,
the one my father called feisty, was Prewitt
in the movie, and in my twelve-year-old conception
of things, in the magical drive-in dark, I knew it
was true: I'd found the man I'd aim to be.
Suddenly, the fact that I could sing meant something,
and one long day of rain my father let me
ease from their even rows his dazzling
collection of records. Among the heavy seventy-eights
of Gershwin and Lanza, I found him there—
Sinatra in a rumpled suit, hands in his pockets, hate
in his eyes, or love, I couldn't tell. He peered
off the jacket with steel in his blood, with style,
while every song was love gone wrong, old tunes
blue with heartbreak. I believed his smile
was deadly, that weakness was ruin.
Five years later, still not disabused
of the cinemascope hokum, it was Sinatra, not me,
flipping off the nightclub bouncer, the fake ID I'd used
slipped neatly into the till. And tonight, twenty
years further into our lives, Sinatra and I have both outlived
those early days. The drive-ins are gone, and Gaslight Square,
and that bouncer, who grinned and shoved
me twice, out the door and against the front wall,
and hit me once so hard in the gut
that I knelt among the sidewalk crowd and cried, all
the night's easy beers boiling out.
There are whole weeks now
when I'm trapped inside the stereo's thrall,
when the old Sinatra convincingly sings how
love goes wrong. A little light turns the walls

golden, I have solitaire and sentiment, whiskey and comfort,
but I wake up empty. Daydreams run
my life now, and I wonder what sort
of man I might've been, what sort I've become.

THE FLIGHT LINE

Summer days that paved world shimmers with heat,
and my father walking the flight line to his car
might be imaginary, a mirage, the wavery light
fluttering his clothes like silks. Behind him
fighters scream far out of proportion
to their size and distance, and the transports
—huge as buildings—rock the earth
as they lumber barely aloft.

It is 1969. After the long drive home
he falls asleep in his chair, the newspaper unfolding
over his lap and legs, ears ringing
in the unreliable silence. He is already half-deaf,
but I want him to hear my rants against the war
his planes are bound for.

Over dinner the TV's roar keeps us quiet.
At right angles to each other
my father and I fume with rage,
my mother and sister tense as cats.
This is how we live the year before I'm drafted,
suffering ourselves and the pretense of meals,
until one night, when the weekly dead are known,
and we are caught, frozen, peering
into the tablecloth's cheerful pattern,
listening against our will to the newsman.
On that night, as on so many others,
I cannot contain myself and lift my eyes and see
my mother, her head bowed, stirring absently at her food,
and then begin the turn toward my father,
prepared again to say what I should not,
to say it and mean it, to spill it out
like bile on the table before us—
my hatred for the nation of my birth.

But this night, when I turn to him
I say nothing. Slowly his head shakes
side to side, his face blank as wind,
and I am so stunned to see him crying
I can say nothing at all
before he is up and leaving the table,
and we are alone with the televised war.

On the screen in black and white, soldiers
my own age speak and grin and bleed.
It is an enormous distance across that room, that house
in the American heartland, miles from the planes,
the shimmering image of the flight line,
those destinations far to the east and exotic. Every day
my father vanishes with his skilled hands,
with the seeds of his sweat, with his sleepiness,
and reappears at dusk and takes his meals
with us—his wife, his daughter, his angry son—
while all night long the planes grind upward.
We must hear them sometimes,
far aloft and rumbling. We lie awake
and dream our thoughts skyward—luck,
refusal, fear, and rage—and believe
now and then they get through, like prayers.
We are alone with ourselves,
our house a small darkness in the greater dark,
from which we might wave our hands bloody
and never be seen.

SIMPLE NUMBERS

We knew nothing of women but spoke of them
in the bluntest particulars, the one girl
there giggling, drawing hard on
the reefer in her hand. In that whirl
of smoke and music, the ceremony we'd gathered for
was simple numbers: a calendar unstrung
across the wall, pictures of the war
clipped from magazines, eleven young
men and a younger girl, her eyes
dull with dope and abandon. Three of us lost that day,
and two of us, if what the TV said wasn't lies,
would be drafted, would take orders, would obey.

Take a boy's few years
in a man's husk, fill him with dying, and set him on
himself in another color, another country, another
world. Three of us lost, and two of us
one by one left for the bedroom and found her there
curled in the covers. Maybe we caressed
her, maybe we touched her in some gentle way for
a moment, and maybe felt in that moment
the blind beginnings of regret, before the smoke-buzz
and beer, the numbers, sent
us on her in the wrong equation we called love.

We believed in nothing but the abacus of hands,
the wealth of muscle, the drum
of our marching hearts, that intoxicating dance
in the problem of numbers, of which we ourselves were the sum.

INVISIBLE MEN

1

For the mile past American Steel
I breathed in my cargo of roses,
but even in that sweetness I could feel
the lung grit and chronic bloody noses
of my childhood. It was my last day
delivering flowers, and the dead man
these were meant to honor couldn't stay
dead in the town he lived in,
where the undertakers all were white.
Like me, doing my buck-an-hour duty,
driving deep into Venice, Illinois, and its blighted
air with a perfect spray of American Beauty
roses, Boston fern, and baby's breath for the casket.
What did I know? I was nineteen, a week
away from the army, and if you'd asked
I'd have just said, "Luck, bad luck,"
and looked away, believing for the moment in flowers.
I don't remember. Maybe I was told
it was all cosmetic, that even after hours
of trying, of dabbing at dead skin as cold
as any, no white man could make a black face
presentable. Maybe I believed that
the way I believed I'd go anyplace
the army sent me, the way I believed what
we'd all been told—dominoes and honor,
fine and fitting things, the old lies.
How could I have known any different? Conned or
gullible, probably both, I honed my eyes
on beer and smoke, my ears ringing
with wild guitars. In Venice that day,
late winter, young black men gathered singing
around trash-can fires, and no one looked my way.

A white boy with a job, a longhair,
I couldn't outshine the package store lights.
I was out of focus in the noxious air,
in March, when not even clouds were white.

2

What is that smell in funeral homes?
formaldehyde? ammonia? Chrysanthemums,
gladiolas, carnations, the roses I followed,
held out before me and nodding like beggars,
like mourners—amen, amen, my steps
murmuring down the carpeted hall. They were
gathered in the chapel, the family I slipped
past, though I felt them watch
while I nestled the casket-piece in place.
Flag-draped and sealed, steel-cold to the touch,
the coffin held a soldier, whose black face
grinned at me from an 8 x 10 portrait.
And what I don't understand today
is how I looked back at him without
so much as a blink, how I eased away,
cool and professional, slowly, making sure
the roses were right, balanced and symmetrical,
how, until I turned toward where
the family waited, I could not tell
they were crying. Silent, emptied, they
didn't look at me at all as I left,
but at one another, or at the plush gray
floor, or at the roses and fern and baby's breath—
expensive, short-lived, and meager. In that air
so full with dying, I moved like a wrist,
like sleep, impossible, invisible, there
and not there, like the people I passed

on the smoke-killed streets of Venice,
like the dead man I looked at but didn't see,
like the country itself imagining a menace
from across the world, while back home we
trucked our darker dead away and paid
ourselves little more than nothing to buy it:
the lie, the dazzling flag, frayed
to the edge of its true colors, white on white on white.

C.O.

We left the quarter peep shows, the lurid skin
magazines and comical, unimaginable toys,
and headed down the block toward the Quakers, a fever in
us from freedom and fear, a pure joy
our first trip away from the army in weeks.
They were American Friends, in a cluttered,
postered storefront, and the fleshy peeks
we'd taken left us shamed and flustered
before their devotion. Out the fly-specked window
and across the street the Alamo hunkered in dust
behind its gate. Our counselors knew the C.O.
route, would mention Canada only if they must,
and showed in their eyes a faith I
imagined as big as Texas. I could just make out
my face reflected in the window, about to cry,
a kid who knew only that he wanted out.

First they told us the rules: you must oppose
all wars and make no distinction between
them. No matter what violence goes
on around you, you must remain passive. Even
if your father is attacked by thugs, you
must say you'd only place your quiet, beatific self
between him and their blows. This is all you can do.
Here the counselors stopped, took from the shelf
the book of regs, and read the army's loaded
catechism, and we nodded and they went on.
But maybe then we daydreamed. Already a code
our fathers knew, and the country, was broken.
I was nineteen years old and could not tell
if I was a coward or a man of conviction,
didn't know if what I feared was a private hell
or the throes of our lovely, miserable nation.

And this is the simple end:
I pleaded the Christianity I've never believed
and got myself out. My American Friend
was a lawyer who drove a Mercedes and grieved
into tears each week at the list of the dead.
There was no sense in anything. And on the day
I got out, I went with Padilla, the Puerto Rican head,
to the quartermaster for paperwork and pay.
Padilla, from New York, beautiful and muscular
and younger than me. We smoked dope
and I woke up chilled, clammy with fear
before the last sergeant of my life. "I hope
you're glad," he said, and I was too high
and frightened to know what he really meant,
but he stamped my papers, paid me, and said good-bye,
then I found Padilla, and we shook hands, and went.

WHAT MY FATHER BELIEVED

Man of his age, he believed in the things
built by men, the miracles of rockets and bombs,
of dams and foundries, the mind-killing
efficiency of assembly lines. And now the boredom
and blankness with which these students respond
to the tale of my father's loss of faith sadden me,
as times before I have saddened myself. Around
the middle of his life, I baited him wildly,
hung in my room the poster of Malcolm X,
whose lips were stilled around a word
that could have been freedom, or fight, or fuck.
I remember the first time I heard
my father say it. We had argued and I thought
I'd won. It was the same awful subject,
the war. I see now it was never how he had fought,
but his countrymen. He said we should not expect
to love war, but to know sometimes there was no way
around it, and I laughed and said, "Just stop."
In his eyes I saw what he couldn't say,
though right as I was, I could not
predict what he muttered. The rage that made
him flush and stutter and sweat was gone,
and only a fool of twenty couldn't see the blade
of pain he suffered, and suffered all along.
What should I say to him today, when the truth
I was so eager to embrace is constantly told,
when the plainness of it rankles like a bad tooth
in our mouths and the students scold
us both as naive and thoughtless. What of Custer?
they ask. What of racism? slavery? the inexorable theft
of every acre of native land? And I can muster
no answer they'll accept, but am left

at the end of class the argument's dull loser,
silent, contemplating the nature of instruction.
My father believed in the nation, I in my father,
a man of whom those students have not the slightest notion.

THE OVERCOAT

The winter sun blinded, glass buildings
repeated the sky and all the endless traffic
trailed plumes of exhaust, white and vanishing.
I'd come out of the store wearing my new coat,
the old one in a box beneath my arm,
when I felt a hand on me.
He was old and white-haired. "I'll pay
you," he said. "I've got furniture to move.
I can't do it myself." Around us
the topcoated businessmen flew about
like leaves and pigeons strutted in the gutters.

I followed him south and east,
out of the glittery district of mirrors,
toward the fleabag hotels by the licorice factory.
The air was camphorous, our breaths flagged out
and sailed away. From a street of dead cars
he led me into a hall, smoke-dark
and redolent of licorice and urine.
Could I really not have known
what he wanted, there in the cold
and filth of that empty room,
when he turned to me and said nothing
but knelt as though to beg, his spotted hands
shivering? In that world unmade of glass
where the sun cannot shine, I knew. In that street,
that building, that brutal hall,
that room in which I gave away
what I had no need for.

THE GRANDMOTHERS   *for Les Barnes*

He thought, this is the way they all are,
the grandmothers, and time is a cancer
we laugh through. He lit her cigarette
and handed it to her over the untouched hospital tray.
Her smile then, her perfect teeth—
they remained while the doctors whittled her away.

Single-lunged and breastless, diabetic and half-blind,
she ruled her house without rules.
Everywhere the heaped junk harbored its rats,
his parents feared tetanus and complained
about the sugar bowl, spoonfully eaten
in the late night TV's blue, blue glow.

One school night she wakened him,
hauled him groggy through rooms of sleep,
through the sleeping rooms, to the back porch,
that blistered ruin, and showed him
the distant storm, lightning's true skewers
and time-lapse thunder, the breeze rich with ozone.

On another, they left the house
carrying his books, his sacked, sweet lunch,
and walked the easy miles to the river,
where they swam utterly naked
and dug for mussels and slept on the beach
all the long night, then walked to school.

Even now, sand in his shoe brings her back,
or the tumble of the clothes dryer
she once let him ride. Lightning too,
and sugar, the wet-rot scent of rivers
and lakes, the moon-shiny swirl in a mussel's shell,
teeth and laughter, a cigarette's undulant smoke.

He thought, now she will die, and watched
the flame ooze slowly down the shaft.
Smoke curled out the tube between her ribs,
and with her free hand she gestured to it,
smiling. He thought, ozone, the ancient air,
the long, long night they must swim through.

OF DIAMONDS

The dew has sown a field of diamonds
behind his house. He warms his hands
on a coffee cup, scans the trails
of deer and elk back into the hills.
Though it is hunting season, they feed
on spent tomatoes in the garden, raid
the high grass of his fencerows.
Some even have come to the house, roses
below a bedroom window cropped away.
He has killed them in the past. Yesterday
the rifle sighted perfectly in, he swore
he'd be ready for half-light, the poor
straggling bull or buck easing off at dawn—
and he was ready, his rifle braced on
a banister, the elegant cross hairs
aligning, dividing the four quarters
of the heart. But something stopped him, kept
his finger still while the world slept
and the deer, oblivious as dew, stood,
then drifted out of sight to the woods.

Now, mid-morning, he is alone
and wondering. The children have gone
to school, his wife—a teacher—to her classes,
and as he watches a hawk pass
over the stubbled furrows, he feels
an overwhelming calm and ease. He will
survive all the seasons he can imagine,
his children will prosper, and the young men
who yearly fall in love with his wife
will know nothing of pain at his expense. If
they dream of her, he will understand.

They are like the deer and elk, walking the land
as though they were invisible, driven
by a hunger they cannot comprehend.
He lives his nights, and theirs
too, breathing in the air
from beloved sleepers, while the earth
is walked by animals unaware of the true worth
of diamonds.

FLIGHT

All morning I have watched the robins
in their courtship flights and dances,
and I admit—before I thought
to come back to bed, to enter again
the orbit of your body
around sleep and dream—

that I thought at first of that man
you know and spoke of last night, a brilliant man,
a scholar, a sinecured and professional thinker,
who did not know and could not believe
there are men and women
who take the Bible as absolute fact.

"Even Jonah?" he asked. "Moses and the Red Sea?"
And he could not understand, and vowed,
you thought, silently, to remain
in all things skeptical, believing nothing
but the dreams of language, the sleep
that is the world we wake to.

What would he have seen in those robins?
What song in their raucous
clacks and jabbers? I believe in
a literal seduction, how undressed of flight
and feathers, that dance
is a language as keen as our own.

I believe when I came to you in your sleep,
when I was long awake, when I roused you half into
the world the robins weave their flights in,

that we too were literally aloft, that I licked awake
the wings from your shoulders, and we turned
and slanted and coasted down the same long breezes

as any birds, swallowed by the air, and believing.

IN THE DARK POOL, FINDING YOU

No lights, no moon, no stars in the mountains,
clouds clearing the night with blackness and an owl
fooling from the pine at the edge of the meadow.
Lover, I am silent in these simmering waters,
the sulphur clouds we breathe are invisible
where you taunted me with nakedness
and swam away in tease. I am blind.

From his low bough bellows the owl, who
sees you, pink in the earth-cooked pool. I would have
eyes like his if I were dreaming, and a voice
to stir the night with, calling where? where?
Instead I am a muskrat, my mop of dark hair
wakelessly moving alleys over the surface
toward where I will find you and gently gnaw

your shoulder, where your skin will nearly squeak.
These are womb-waters, I say aloud, and the owl
goes quiet. I say I am a seed for you,
hoping you'll giggle, hoping somehow the water will
quicken and I'll know what corner you hide in,
what loop you swim around me, what vague dream
the eyes concoct in the lead an owl can live in.

Light is a trick of luck the blind man learns
to live without. Lover, here are my hands
imagining you, all swells and softnesses lightly giving.
In these waters, body-warm, I can make up
where you are, and it will be true.
This is love's skill and power, as real as the owl,
high in the pine, and dining on imaginary mice.

ONIONS

A rooster pheasant crows in the gully
out back, calls his hens, and they file
uneasily beneath the fence, across
the garden, and into the thicket
of star thistle and sage. The cat can't believe
his luck, stalks, then stalls at the sheer
numbers—twelve, sixteen, twenty-one
nervous, low-walking birds—there, everywhere,
then gone. I am on the porch
braiding onions, turning them,
rubbing them up like baseballs,
and the skins fall at my feet in a fluttery pile.
Every tree is losing its leaves, a dry
and skeletal snow, and the horse chestnuts fall
like bombs. The yard is rumpled with buckeyes.
Because it is autumn, because she is pregnant,
due, weary in her bones, beautiful
but feeling frumpy, my wife sleeps
in the living room, inside the heartbeat strike
of the pendulum clock, and dreams
she is making a baby from scratch,
a nubbin of flesh, a sphere around it—bone-colored,
translucent—then another, and another, shaped by her
hands, while outside all the air is
flushed with the scent of onions,
and the strands, a dozen each, hang
from the eaves of the porch until I move them
to the cellar, where they will remain for months.

A MEMORY OF GARLIC   *for Robert Coker Johnson*

Across the pale gray otherworldly umbras
shed by lights in the hospital parking lot,
over the lemony chevrons of pavement stripes
and into the shaded apartment house entry
as gold as the heart of a squash,
along the creaking sepia corridor,
a banister rising above us
and number 2-B aglow in the distance,
we are drawn by the aura of garlic.

For in a drift of papery husks
our friend has labored all afternoon,
until the bowl before him filled
as though with popcorn, that he might take
cool hand- after handful and unload them—
the moon slivers and ghostly shadows
of river-polished rocks—fifty cloves each
in four emptied birds, to simmer and stew
in the sweet, eye-watering, oven darkness.

And though you are pregnant, you enter
willingly into this autumn feast—a little
brown rice tinctured by soy, the year's last
barely turned tomatoes, and the camphorous flesh
of garlic-seething chickens. Out of the carcasses
the cloves tumble like half-formed eggs,
silvered, approaching translucence, butter-soft
and mild as this perfect September night.
He and I scoop them from the platter, and we eat.

Later, when we have said our good-byes and lingered,
because this feast of garlic is our last,
because in a week our friend will leave—

as he must—when we have swum
from that current of richness and scent,
when I have become because of this meal
his magical twin, and he has become mine,
and the soul of this night unravels into other smells,
each one isolate and fading, our homeward steps

past parking lot lights grown huge as moons,
then you will take my hand and stop me
and we will embrace in some dark side street,
your belly swollen with its egg of new skin,
the wind all around us miserably clear
but your hair an airy cloud of garlic,
and my stunned, redolent body
a furnace from within, so many days smoldering
then flaring in a quarter moon's clove of smoke.

RAVENS AT DEER CREEK

Something's dead in that stand of fir
one ridge over. Ravens circle and swoop
above the trees, while others
swirl up from below, like paper scraps
blackened in a fire. In the mountains
in winter, it's true: death is a joyful flame,
those caws and cartwheels pure celebration.
It is a long, snowy mile I've come
to see this, thanks to dumb luck or grace.
I meant only a hard ski through powder,
my pulse in my ears, and sweat, the pace
like a mainspring, my breath louder and louder
until I stopped, body an engine
ticking to be cool. And now the birds.
I watch them and think, maybe I have seen
these very ones, speaking without words,
clear-eyed and clerical, ironic, peering in at me
from the berm of snow outside my window,
where I sprinkled a few crumbs of bread. We
are neighbors in the neighborhood of silence.
They've accepted my crumbs, and when the fire was hot
and smokeless huddled in ranks against
the cold at the top of the chimney. And they're not
without gratitude. Though I'm clearly visible
to them now, they swirl on and sing,
and if, in the early dusk, I should fall
on my way back home and—injured, weeping—
rail against the stars and the frigid night
and crawl a while on my hopeless way
then stop, numb, easing into the darkening white
like a candle, I know they'll stay

with me, keeping watch, moving limb to limb,
angels down Jacob's ladder, wise
to the moon, and waiting for me, simple as sin,
that they may know the delicacy of my eyes.

THE BIG DIPPER

It is winter, we are driving at night,
my young son and I, when he sees
the first constellation of his life,
sees it really, clearly, peering
into the northerly sky over the emptiness
of central Idaho, the road glazed
along the river, the river star-washed, vivid
with its own constellations of rapid and wave,
sees it before I do, too keen
on the deadly highway, the subzero winds,
the arctic darkness hauled down by stars,
sees it and calls out its shape—
"like a big spoon, and there's its handle"—
and I know that I have told him before,
knelt behind him and pointed past his shoulder
to the bail that is a bear, delicate rust-ridden
dipper leaking star- and moonlight on us,
which he sees as well, and feels
grown-up about—this little knowledge
of the infinite I smile to understand,
seeing in his innocence and wonder my own,
which I hold out to him as though it were something
he might guide his life by, as though beyond
this treacherous, iced-over highway
there existed something I was bright enough to follow
on the long drive to where
we're headed, toward home, that cold house
dusted under hoarfrost, under the North Star.

BODY AND SOUL

Yellow with newness, the other saxophones
throw rings of light across the auditorium ceiling,
but the brass of my son's horn has richened
to melted butter, an inch-deep translucence
on a bell of gold. I am straining to hear
his note among the many, the melody
rising out of flatness, the tempo lost
among the clatter of young tapping feet.

It looked decrepit at first, here and there
the chrome keys showing a dingy, plumber's brass,
two buttons emptied of mother of pearl.
But the horn man fixed all that:
polish and pearly disks and most of all
the way he breathed it into life
that day we picked it up.
From dozens of great, cloth-covered hooks
hung an orchestra of silence,
saxophones of every pitch and size,
the ungainly trombones and sinewy trumpets.
He sat on a padded barstool and played
"Body and Soul," slow and blue as night,
breath-soft but truly singing
in the bell of every idle horn.

Through the eastern window, sun shone
on his torch, his precision tools,
the floor all around him a litter of felt
and metal shavings, the stilled splashes of solder.
It was cathedral light and nightclub music
when he finished and spoke to my son
of his favorite players—Parker and Pepper,

113

their true hearts and perfect lungs
exchanging the night air with angels.

*

Neither of us speaks on the way home,
but in the middle of the living-room floor
he swabs his horn and reshines it,
nestles it in its battered brown case,
and looks. He points to a key, pokes it twice,
and says, "This is one the horn man fixed."
He pokes it again and again
and suddenly I know what he's thinking.
That tune the horn man played
wasn't a song at all, but something magic.
The way it swirled in the empty bells
had less to do with breath than wind,
the sort of wind that never wakes you
but brings some dream, in the scent
of flowers or the newly chilled air,
that for all your life you'll never forget.

The truth is, I'll be surprised
if music is his dream. For the moment
it's his mild affliction. He borrows Art Pepper
from my pile of tapes, and I hear moments later
the first plaintive notes of "Body and Soul."
It's late, he's a boy in a small American town
in love with believing, and despite anything
I might say, believes he's alone in the world.

                              his pansies drink
the darkness down, replenishing their purples.
It is a country tune, fit for clogging,
for hobnobbing with a jug of shine,
neither lovely nor mournful, but the wind is
in a minor key, and the sliver of moon
behind the house fails to lighten where we are.
Faintly, his cigarette glows a slow
exaggerated pulse. It never leaves his mouth.
He has four daughters, all lovely, all newly women.
Out front the youngest one giggles and squirms
away from the boy who would touch her, but not so far
he can't. Back here, her father's reached
that part of the song where the tempo leans
forward into recklessness, and even though it's dark
I can feel his concentration, his care, I can sense
his willingness to let the tune take him
into that kingdom of blind men and saints,
wounded gawkers at stars, moon-stunned children
wild in bodies they entirely are feeling.
Now the wind picks up, now the tempo.
The ember of his cigarette brightens
until I can almost make out his face,
but not his hands, working above the supple strings,
making the guitar—from its elegant, rich-
scented chamber, its smooth grain and slim-waisted body—sing.

PARKING

Today I live where I have always been
an adult, where I have always kept the same
job, known the same friends, driven
the same streets. What is it
that is not in me now, that has not been
in me for many years, that rigid
sense of direction that led me
always to where they were parked,
the coupled cars, bumper to bumper,
or side by side, windows glazed,
sweat-ridden, sodden with fumbling
and passion.

        Where are they?
Here, in the empty West, are they lost
so easily, so easily vanished into forests,
arroyos, the blind rutted ranch roads
to nowhere? Or were we—miners'
children, blessed in beer and whiskey, salted
early by the salty tongues of grandmothers—
allowed a wilderness our earth
could no longer afford? The times,
have they just got used to it all,
the motel lots each Saturday night filling
with jalopies.

        I would not trade
the familiar bedroom, the creak of spring,
the ease of middle age. But
somewhere I want to believe
the cars still rumble into place,
those hot rods, the lucky ramblers
in the station wagons of their fathers.
I want to believe the teeth still chatter,

from winter cold or summer passion.
I want to believe in an ardor as keen
as the homing pigeon's, who reconnoiters, banks,
lands, and coos like a fool in the dark.

DUST

From the hard-rutted, high-line road, the dust
billowed up like spindrift behind us,
a skin-colored cloud slowly ghosting away.
I loved the dry poultice a single summer day
could be in the mountains, even these mountains,
heavily timbered and ripped again and again
for their logs. I loved the dust as fine
as flour, settled in wind rows and sometimes—
in a low, exposed spot on a south-facing slope—
drifted over the road like a waterless pool, a swamp
of bones and dead men's breath, untracked
and hot as fresh ash. And it is a fact
that we usually exploded into such places
like children, laughing, while the dust chased
us along the road. But there was one
dry wash we stopped for: lake-sized, the pure dun
from moth wings troweled smooth as glass.
It was a miracle we waded into past
our knees, a hot bath of earth you swore
we could swim through, so we did, and it poured
into us like sun, like music, and we rose
on that other shore changed, our clothes,
our hair, our hands, our lips altogether earth.
That day, we learned again the easy worth
of motion, the truck a dead sea away,
idling, shimmery with heat, and in every way
the antithesis of mountains, their imperceptible dance,
their purity of waiting, those certainties we see as chance.

—in memory of Richard Hugo

Salt-dazed in fresh water, he eats
nothing but the miles upstream, lame
ladders over dams and the silty back-
waters behind them, slack, brackish, and dull.

Some believe in the hatchery, some
in the river, but each believes in the code
for home. He makes his way shimmering,
all iridescence and muscle, a fog-bound apple

in the uphill world. His convex eye
beholds us, our emissaries of feather and steel,
and he strikes—no reason but the hell
of distance, the cantankerous, tiresome way.

If we are lucky, we love enough
to let him go. Unhooked, lightly held
near the surface of a pool, he'll sway
and pulse, drift and flex.

And in our numb fingers we'll feel him
come alive, the coil and re-coil
of heart and hard flesh, the slick shot snaked
toward oblivion, that pure dream of home.

THE WHITE CAT

1

He swore this once he'd believe in magic,
that over miles and the crackling neurons of air
he'd know the instant his father died.
Under the same moon they were
constantly in touch—a chill in the August sun,
the white telepathy of snow: he would know,
he would know . . .

                    The earth itself
might show it, willows nodding, the hue
of late sun in a sagebrush gully.
I will taste his absence, he said, in water
or whiskey, smell it on the neck
of the newborn child. I will know.

2

That night he couldn't decipher the dream,
there was nothing, only darkness and his name,
its childish diminutive, hung in the air
like smoke. Had he heard it at all, rasped
once, or just the neighbors' rusty gate
swung wide in a wind?

                    He rose, walked
to the window, and listened. Streetlights
flickered through leaves, a white cat
padded down his driveway and stopped.
There was something in the bushes it saw,
and now it waited, still as stone.
Still as a root, it waited.

NIGHT CALLS

Locusts

No explanation will suffice, no dictionary
description nor entomological chart. Nothing
can keep him from dreaming the night's blue mouth,
the swirl, the rowel of locusts inside.
He awakens, eases up the sash closed earlier
against the noise, presses his boy's soft cheek
to the screen's crosshatch and rust, and listens.
His lips begin to form the syllable,
the round wow and whine of locusts—
dream-breath of all the empty world
he lives in, and speaks to, and loves.

The Midnight Whistle

On the drive across town he hears it.
He moves his one hand easily over the wheel,
with the other pulls the girl closer,
and she curls against his shoulder and side:
now the night possesses a little magic.
On the radio a DJ's voice drops
toward hot oil and smoke, the thrum
from the car's engine is power he controls.
He drives toward the country, the girl's
house and restless father, amazed
how after midnight, at fifty miles per hour,
the locusts still are a constant collective voice,
though now he can hear every mile
of the way a single blare louder than the others.

121

His Wife
At the edge of sleep, in the wash of the covers
he hears it, her sigh—half breath, half song—
and he is awake. For how long does he wait
on the far side of their bed? Minutes? Hours?
Then something pulls him on, the moon,
the memory of years before, in the half-dark
of his old car, her eyes moving him at will,
and he slides across the bed, magically
glides there as softly as the flow
of honey. Then he is against her,
holding her, easing her from sleep
as carefully as once he held her face in his hands
in the front seat of his car, and drew from her
that song of breath, that sigh he will always know.

His Children
In his dream it is the ruined farm
windmill, or his daughter, the little girl's breath
in sickness laborious and wet. He rises
to see and follows his hands through the darkness.
At the far end of the hall, the girl's room
bronzed from the pumpkin night-light,
thick with a vaporizer's fog. Next door
the older brother behind his lock and sneer,
dreaming impossible women. And there,
in the hallway of his mortgaged house,
in the narrow place where they all meet
and pass—his wife, his children, his local
unlistening self—he lies down to sleep
and hear. On one side the bruising silence,
on the other the tiny and regular rasps,
and the damp wind blowing into the hall,
making nothing better.

122

His Heart

Not insomnia, but the body's noisy sleep.
First he is aware of his breathing, that it is
something he must address—
like a pull-up bar, his hands white with rosin.
And when he rolls onto his back,
folds his hands across his chest, his heart
is marching there, muscling the dull limbs
and weary brain hard toward tomorrow.
He looks into the air above him: nothing.
He listens for any sign from the outside
world, any call but the code
his life is measured by, the rhythm
he dances to, that monotonous thump
he curses and yearns for.

THE SCAR

In her backpack the baby sputters and cheers
because I'm sitting on the sloped, grassy shore,
because her feet touch the ground. She pushes hard,
we rock. Her older brother flings bread
to the ducks on the pond, the few geese
honk and glower. It is days like these—
deep into autumn but warm as July,
the easy breezes and perfect sky
everywhere around us—when I almost believe
the world can be healed. And maybe it's the waves
from the paddling ducks that bring
the gunnysack of drowned cats rising
to the surface like a dream.
Maybe it's not cats at all, just some
fool's load of trash foolishly tossed here.
But the ducks give it a wide berth, and now they're
moving away, though my son keeps flinging
bread and the baby goes on jabbering
and the open weave of the burlap gradually breaks
the surface, and when it does the stench takes
the wind away and the sun shines
on our leaving, the sun in its blue dome,
the dying sun and a jet plane
leaving its smoke-like scar
silver in the autumn light, far, far
above our leaving, that scar, there,
unraveling already in cold, pure air.

SHRAPNEL

"Shrapnel," he says to me, "seems wrong,"
for the filament of steel that tore his spine
is nothing like what the word suggests.
Tiny, elegant, almost blunt,
it is his amulet in a film can,
each day taken out and caressed,
worn smooth and shiny as a bearing.

I have come to know him
through our morning walks, mine afoot,
his in a wheelchair with a shepherd dog
called Hue. Just as you probably suspect
he wears an army field jacket and a beard.
With an old racket he hammers a tennis ball
half a block for his dog to chase.

For a year now it is I
who have hit the ball for Hue,
while his master visits the naturopath
for herbal packs and high colonics,
his legs, he swears, more alive than ever,
shimmering in his lap with cold fire,
a sweet and unlocalized tingling.

He has asked me, politely, almost shyly,
for poems, and I give them to him—
Wilfred Owen and Weigl—
and he reads them on the spot,
slowly and carefully, like love letters
or contracts. Always, when he is finished,
he murmurs and folds them away in a pocket.

Sometimes we talk about the weather
or women, and then I have to leave
for school, so we wave and go our opposite ways,
he with his dog who loves him
and I with my messages of art
and the word. From the back porch
of his little house he watches

high school boys batter themselves silly
on the practice football field,
and I enter this new brick building,
stiflingly hot, ragged with conversations,
and stride to the front of the room
and survey the young faces, already bored,
and find, for some reason, I cannot speak.

I don't blame them, you know.
It must look those mornings
as though I've lost my mind, or my way.
I want to tell them sometimes I died
in the war I refused to go near.
Truly, I am ashamed
for my life, my lies, my legs.

Today, we will speak of Robert Frost,
his ambitions, his perfections.
They have read a few poems
and I have a film to show,
but as always I begin with a word,
something plucked from the blustery fall air
for no good reason but the mind

and its hard affiliations with the world.
I am quite entertaining some days,
going on about the harsh aesthetics of phlegm
or the mouthy succulence of undulate.
They know what's coming. I walk
back and forth, back and forth,
until the right word comes, and changes nothing.

LIGHT AFTER LIGHT

—in memory of
Rudolph Valentino York,
atomic veteran

1

Out of the corner of his eye it looked
like a carp, one of those gold-sided monsters
spinning in the shallows, a boil of scales and mud.
Or it was light, the sun a blonde scallop shimmering
over waves. He scanned the far shore and dreamed
another year, the nettles there and gnarled arms of thistles.
With two thousand other sailors he'd swept
hot dust the bomb test blew and basked
barefooted in the sweet Pacific sun.

And he knew the stillness well,
how smoke soothed his single lung and the miles
back to his junk-strewn shanty,
where the cool, bottled air remained.
One handed he'd rolled a joint, driven
the red clay Oklahoma back road to nowhere,
this cattailed, duckweedy slough.

In the light after light in the slant
toward dusk, he saw what it was and froze,
his hand spun limp off the slick-turning reel,
the wake of his line gone rippling through weeds.
She was blonde and bound in wire,
faceup and openmouthed. Already
the algae mottled her flesh.

2

Look at him, across his kitchen table.
He's barechested, a new growth lolls
below the scar on his ribs. His skin's
so leathery and dark the tattoos of his youth
barely show. What can you say to him here,

while the TV earsplittingly blathers and coffee boils
in a tin can on the stove?

                              That day he found her, when
he began to breathe again, the air was death-tinted,
but rich, a kind of humus in the wind. He turned,
broke his line, and left. He never said a word.

And now you're in it, that room
a dying man has come to, where the televised light flashes
on the little he owns: fishing tackle,
tools, sweet air in blue rented bottles.
And the light he watched one day
long ago was someone else's crime,
all the waters lit up and dying.

Finally, the TV's off, that Oklahoma heat
screws down. The story you've heard
lingers in the air like humidity
and the barking dogs of shantytown sound
musical as angels. You take a deep breath,
and out of the corner of your eye
see your own car, shiny and air-conditioned,
sleek for the long drive away.

In the sun and wet haze I am walking
a little north of west, my dark glasses wrong
for the icy finality of the place. No one's talking,
but a man in fatigues sings a quiet song
I can't remember, and I can't say why
I'm here. Like everyone else, to read
the names and finger the ones I knew, to cry
a little as I descend to the heart of the war. Perhaps I need
this pain. By the year I was drafted
refusals were common, a whole barracks of us waited
for word and could not believe the war had lasted
so long. We cursed, we thought we hated
everything about the land we'd learned at last to see.
And in the years since then, nothing has changed
my mind, nothing has made me
believe the lies or the truth rearranged
to suit a few men in charge. And what little I know
to be true is the names on this wedge of wall,
on the eastern brink of a nation that will not show
its blunders and murders and fools. I love all
these men, because they are dead,
because their deaths called out to me
warnings few among the living could have said,
and I believed them absolutely.
Should you go there, know this: that the walk
from the center of that wall is not the same
as any climb anywhere else. You walk,
but heavily, slowly, filled with the absent weight of names.

CAMPING

I see my father camping, twenty-seven years
ago grappling inside the canvas gullet of a tent
he made with Harvey Winkleman, in their spare time,
working lunches and breaks, sewing a shell
around a skeleton of coded tubing,
between parachutes and the fancified seats
of the personal planes of generals,
every day through winter and spring assembling
a camouflaged and round-shouldered pyramid
in which they would sleep with their families
for two fleeting weeks of summer vacation in Yellowstone
or the Ozarks, or alongside some newly made lake,
behind a dam, a smooth and miraculous monolith
made also by men, men like them,
who could imagine one flood controlling all others,
who could see themselves as well in the summers
upcoming, camping: the laughter of children
hiding in the woods or swimming in the shallows,
wives lying on the docks in the sun
or stirring some stew, squatting in the blue smoke
from the campfire.

        I see my father camping,
calling over twenty-seven years for one
then another and another of those numerically coded poles,
all twenty-eight of them, his voice rising
toward madness, the clink again and again
of the flashlight falling from his shaking hands,
the wild shaking of the canvas walls,
shaking of the pine boughs by the wind,
and my shivering mother and sister, still
in the car and huddled up front around the heater.
I see us speaking little over dinner,

cooked and eaten in the meager light
of the ancient Coleman lantern, the dinner instantly cold,
my mother shocked again by my father's temper,
my father raging toward fun, believing
like so many of his countrymen in that time
of blind prosperity, in the things
he could fashion with his hands and mind,
in the wisdom of what came down to him
from the ones he'd elected, from the ones
who'd won the war.

                      I see my father camping
today, still devoted in his way to manufacture
and technology. Carefully he backs his trailer into place,
carefully he cranks his jacks, eases
the bubble of his level toward center.
He is old, he says, and deserves these
comforts, but I do not believe him.
He has always deserved his life, like the rest of us,
and now he walks with my mother along the trails
in the woods, across the beaches, and they look
like lovers. We're warred out,
he says, and he means his country,
and his rages he confines to a muttered obscenity,
a shrug of disgust for what passes these days for wisdom.
Retired, he thinks of his occupation as camper,
listener, and he understands at last what brought him
out of town. We look at one another through the smoke
of the campfire. We do not speak.
It is the quiet he strains to hear,
the noisy silence of another world he has grown nearer to
this late in his life.
Listen, another day is almost gone.

132

THE WISHING TREE

My son left his notebook on the picnic table
and took his rod and reel down
to the river to fish. A little breeze blew
the pages over, blew smoke my way
from the fire we had drunk our coffee and chocolate by.
I was washing the breakfast dishes,
enjoying my hands in the hot sudsy water
and the steam from them rising as I dried
metal plates and wooden spoons and laid
the iron skillet top down on a flat stone
by the fire. I even enjoyed just sitting there,
watching grouse blunder stupidly out of the brush
and into our campsite, enjoyed just looking
at the drawings and stories in my son's notebook—
the great trout and sheer unclimbable mountains, the sun
with its penicilled-in, symmetrical rays, the tales
about football and horses and school,
and an old Indian man who found a tree for wishes.

And now I wish I had stopped looking, and loafing,
wish I'd risen and wrestled on my waders.
I wish I'd left camp and seen my son at the river
hold up a lunker trout, gingerly, by the jaw—
the way I'd taught him. I wish
I'd tossed away my coffee and gone,
but I didn't. I stayed there, looking
at a thing he'd drawn, a picture of rockets,
rows of them, ranks and ranks of them
like the fences from suburban backyards
foreshortened by a telephoto lens,
and fire, everywhere flame and smoke,
ruins and rubble, everywhere
but a white sphere of peace, a circle at the bottom of the page,

in which two people played catch.
In their little space, they were all
out of proportion, as large as the rockets
that surrounded them, and their mouths
simple, straight, bold lines—not the usual smiles—
as though the game they played required the strictest concentration,
as though for some reason they could never
let the ball not be caught, as though everything
depended on them, everything—
and in the picture, it did, it did.

Acknowledgments for *Moon in a Mason Jar*

Some of these poems have appeared previously in the following
publications:

The American Poetry Review: "The Beliefs of a Horse," "Mowing"
The Chariton Review: "The Skull of a Snowshoe Hare"
The Chowder Review: "Weaver of Wind," "Yard Work"
Cimarron Review: "Lover of Fire"
Crab Creek Review: "A Photo of Immigrants"
The Georgia Review: "Torch Songs"
GiltEdge: "Running in Your Sleep"
The Kenyon Review: "The Crèche"
Manhattan Poetry Review: "The Sound Barrier"
The Missouri Review: "Appalonea"
The Montana Review: "The Glow," "The Leaning House," "Termites"
New England Review & Breadloaf Quarterly: "Collection," "Pheasant
    Hunting," "Star Dust"
The Ohio Review: "Moonlight: Chickens on the Road"
Partisan Review: part 1 of "Aubade for Mothers"
Quarterly West: "Fireflies," part 3 of "Aubade for Mothers," Heart
    Attack"
The Seattle Review: "The Owl"
Western Humanities Review: "The Bees," "Nightcrawlers"

"Heart Attack" and "Mowing" appeared in the *Anthology of Magazine
Verse and Yearbook of American Poetry* (Beverly Hills, Calif.: Monitor
Book Co., 1984). Several of these poems appeared in the chapbook *The
Glow* (Missoula, Mont.: Owl Creek Press, 1982).

The epigraphs for parts 1–3 are taken from: "A Clear Midnight," by Walt
Whitman, *Leaves of Grass and Selected Prose* (New York: Modern
Library, 1950); Rainer Maria Rilke, letter to Polish translator Witold von
Hulewicz, December 22, 1923, quoted in *Sonnets*, trans. M. D. Herter
Norton (New York: W. W. Norton, 1942); "Summer Wish," by Louise
Bogan, *The Blue Estuaries* (New York: Farrar, Straus & Giroux, 1968).

The author would like to express his gratitude for fellowship grants from
the National Endowment for the Arts in 1978 and 1984, which allowed
him the time to write many of the poems here included.

Acknowledgments for *What My Father Believed*

Some of these poems have appeared previously in the following publications:

CutBank: "Steelhead"

The Georgia Review: "Economics"

The Gettysburg Review: "Ravens at Deer Creek"

The Iowa Review: "Parking"

The Kenyon Review: "Sinatra"

The Missouri Review: "The Big Dipper"

New England Review & Bread Loaf Quarterly: "The Wishing Tree"

The New Virginia Review: "The Overcoat," "The Scar," "The White Cat"

Northern Lights: "His Father's Whistle"

The Pacific Review: "In the Dark Pool, Finding You"

Palouse Journal: "Onions"

Poetry: "American Manhood," "Camping," "C.O.," "For the Last Summer," "What My Father Believed"

Poetry Northwest: "Dust," "The Grandmothers"

Shenandoah: "Body and Soul," "Night Calls," "Night Rising," "Shrapnel"

Virginia Quarterly Review: "Invisible Men"

Witness: "Light after Light"

Yellow Silk: "Flight"

"Flight" and "In the Dark Pool, Finding You" appeared in the chapbook *In the Dark Pool* (Lewiston, Idaho: Confluence Press, 1987).

Moon in a Mason Jar
Robert Wrigley (1986)

Lower-Class Heresy
T. R. Hummer (1987)

Poems: New and Selected
Frederick Morgan (1987)

Furnace Harbor: A Rhapsody of the North Country
Philip D. Church (1988)

Bad Girl, with Hawk
Nance Van Winckel (1988)

Blue Tango
Michael Van Walleghen (1989)

Eden
Dennis Schmitz (1989)

Waiting for Poppa at the Smithtown Diner
Peter Serchuk (1990)

Great Blue
Brendan Galvin (1990)

What My Father Believed
Robert Wrigley (1991)

Something Grazes Our Hair
S. J. Marks (1991)

Walking the Blind Dog
G. E. Murray (1992)

The Sawdust War
Jim Barnes (1992)

The God of Indeterminacy
Sandra McPherson (1993)

Off-Season at the Edge of the World
Debora Greger (1994)

Counting the Black Angels
Len Roberts (1994)

Oblivion
Stephen Berg (1995)

To Us, All Flowers Are Roses
Lorna Goodison (1995)

Honorable Amendments
Michael S. Harper (1995)

Points of Departure
Miller Williams (1995)

Dance Script with Electric Ballerina
Alice Fulton (reissue, 1996)

To the Bone: New and Selected Poems
Sydney Lea (1996)

Floating on Solitude
Dave Smith (3-volume reissue, 1996)

Bruised Paradise
Kevin Stein (1996)

Walt Whitman Bathing
David Wagoner (1996)

Rough Cut
Thomas Swiss (1997)

Paris
Jim Barnes (1997)

The Ways We Touch
Miller Williams (1997)

NATIONAL POETRY SERIES

Eroding Witness
Nathaniel Mackey (1985)
Selected by Michael S. Harper

Palladium
Alice Fulton (1986)
Selected by Mark Strand

Cities in Motion
Sylvia Moss (1987)
Selected by Derek Walcott

The Hand of God and a Few Bright Flowers
William Olsen (1988)
Selected by David Wagoner

The Great Bird of Love
Paul Zimmer (1989)
Selected by William Stafford

Stubborn
Roland Flint (1990)
Selected by Dave Smith

The Surface
Laura Mullen (1991)
Selected by C. K. Williams

The Dig
Lynn Emanuel (1992)
Selected by Gerald Stern

My Alexandria
Mark Doty (1993)
Selected by Philip Levine

The High Road to Taos
Martin Edmunds (1994)
Selected by Donald Hall

Theater of Animals
Samn Stockwell (1995)
Selected by Louise Glück

The Broken World
Marcus Cafagña (1996)
Selected by Yusef Komunyakaa

Nine Skies
A. V. Christie (1997)
Selected by Sandra McPherson

OTHER POETRY VOLUMES

Local Men and *Domains*
James Whitehead (1987)

Her Soul beneath the Bone:
Women's Poetry on Breast Cancer
Edited by Leatrice Lifshitz (1988)

Days from a Dream Almanac
Dennis Tedlock (1990)

Working Classics: Poems on
Industrial Life
*Edited by Peter Oresick and
Nicholas Coles* (1990)

Hummers, Knucklers, and Slow
Curves: Contemporary Baseball
Poems
Edited by Don Johnson (1991)

The Double Reckoning of
Christopher Columbus
Barbara Helfgott Hyett (1992)

Selected Poems
Jean Garrigue (1992)

New and Selected Poems, 1962-92
Laurence Lieberman (1993)

The Dig and *Hotel Fiesta*
Lynn Emanuel (1994)

For a Living: The Poetry of Work
*Edited by Nicholas Coles and
Peter Oresick* (1995)

The Tracks We Leave: Poems on
Endangered Wildlife of North
America
Barbara Helfgott Hyett (1996)

Peasants Wake for Fellini's
Casanova and Other Poems
*Andrea Zanzotto; edited and
translated by John P. Welle and
Ruth Feldman; drawings by
Federico Fellini and Augusto
Murer* (1997)

Moon in a Mason Jar and *What My
Father Believed*
Robert Wrigley (1997)